HEALTHY BUSINESS

The Natural Practitioner's Guide To Success

by Madeleine Harland and Glen Finn

Published by
Hyden House Ltd.
Little Hyden Lane
Clanfield
Hampshire PO8 ORU
Great Britain

First published 1990
© 1990 Madeleine Harland and Glen Finn

Typeset by Barbara James, Rowlands Castle, Hants
Printed by Biddles Ltd., Guildford, Surrey

British Library Cataloguing in Publication Data
Harland, Madeleine, 1958-
   Healthy business ; the natural practitioner's guide to success.
   1.Great Britain. Alternative medicine
   I. Title II. Finn, Glen 1953-
   615.5

ISBN 1 85623 000 7

CONTENTS

Acknowledgements   xi
Foreword   xiii
Introduction   xv

Chapter One   1
VOCATION VERSUS BUSINESS ACUMEN

Orthodox and natural medicine: Uneasy bedfellows? Prevention rather than cure. Working outside the mainstream. A conflict between business and healing. The ethics and practice of charging fees.

Chapter Two   9
WORKING FROM HOME

THE ADVANTAGES:
Inexpensive option which is intimate, relaxed and homely. Your partner can act as receptionist.
THE DISADVANTAGES:
Setting up the room. Family. Animals. Amateur image. Security and theft. Accusations of assault. Obscene and threatening telephone calls. Privacy.
OTHER CONSIDERATIONS:
What you need to work from home. Telephone. Answer phone. Waiting room. Overheads. 'Change of use'. Capital gains tax.

Chapter Three   20
RENTING TIME IN A CLINIC

THE ADVANTAGES:
Low overheads. Renting the time you need. Building up slowly. Referrals to and from other practitioners. Support and professional stimulation from other practitioners. Not being isolated. Self doubt and confidence. Clinical and professional atmosphere. Credibility of working with other established practitioners. Reputation (good and bad) by association. Image. Goodwill of established therapists. Buffer between you and your patients.

THE DISADVANTAGES:
No control over rent increases. Contractual obligations. Limited say on decoration and room layout etc. Personality and professional differences with other practitioners.
OTHER CONSIDERATIONS:
As patients build up you may run out of time and space. A note to fledgling practitioners.

Chapter Four   29
BUYING A CLINIC WITH A PATIENT LIST
THE ADVANTAGES:
Instant patients. Excellent way to expand existing business or start from scratch if you have the capital. Inheriting goodwill and reputation by association. Credibility: therapist who is selling is entrusting you with his patient list. Change over time with advice from established therapist.
THE DISADVANTAGES:
Requires confidence to take on full time practice. Inevitable loss of some patients loyal to departing practitioner. Initial outlay is expensive. Practice may be shaped in a way you do not want to work. Prescribing or therapy techniques may differ. Compromises may be required to suit existing patients. Inheriting a bad reputation. A difference in philosophy or religion between previous and successive practitioners.
OTHER CONSIDERATIONS:
Getting to know the practitioner you are taking over from. Sitting in on consultations before taking over. Valuing the practice and example. Letter of introduction and example. Inheriting stock, remedies, accounts systems, furniture etc. Few hidden expenses.

Chapter Five   38
LEASING PREMISES
THE ADVANTAGES:
Ability to bring in other practitioners. Cost sharing. Colleagues standing in as receptionists for each other in the early days. Joint publicity lectures. Exhibitions and courses.
THE DISADVANTAGES:
Expensive option. Paying rent. Vulnerable to landlord's whims. Reliance on other practitioners.
OTHER CONSIDERATIONS:
Being the boss. Housecalls. Competition from other practitioners. A note on appearance.

Chapter Six   43
BUYING A LONG LEASE
    Multi-therapy clinics. 'Change of use' and the planning
    authorities. Parking facilities. Mortgages. Limited companies.
    Partnerships. Partnership agreements. Solicitors. Case history.
    Design. Decoration and layout. Tiny terrors and teethmarks.

Chapter Seven   51
MONEY, MONEY, MONEY!
    Borrowing money. Business plans and example. Profit forecasts
    and example. Cashflow charts and example. How to approach
    your bank manager. Obtaining a loan. Small business loan.
    Property finance and business mortgages. Free banking.
    Accounts and your accountant. Business accounts and example.
    Earning under £10,000 a year. What you can claim on the
    business. National Insurance contributions. VAT. What are you
    worth?

Chapter Eight   75
SELLING YOUR WARES
    Effective marketing and PR. Word of mouth. Business cards.
    Letter head. Image. Printing and printers. Brass and other kinds
    of plaque. Getting known: free PR. Lectures. Organisations to
    approach. Addresses. Advertising. Local newspapers. Magazines.
    Writing sales copy and advertisments. The 'AIDA' principle.
    Yellow Pages. Teaching courses. Adult Education courses. Using
    Direct Mail. Using computers and word processors.

Chapter Nine   86
THE SECRET WAY TO SUCCESS
    Believing in yourself. Confidence. Self assessment. Positivity and
    other techniques. Goal setting. Imagery. Visualisation. Creating
    your future. Esoteric PR.

Chapter Ten   92
PROFILE OF A PRACTITIONER
    Image and appearance. What type of practitioner are you? The
    importance of mixing with other practitioners. Beware of gurus.

Chapter Eleven   96
TROUBLESHOOTING
    What can go wrong? Impractical overgenerosity.
    Mismanagement of capital. Tying up money in stock. PR checks:
    are you doing enough? High overheads. Scruffy premises.
    Problems with your receptionist and how to solve them.
    Housecalls.

Chapter Twelve   101
DIFFICULT COLLEAGUES
Partnership agreements. Working with friends. Constructive plain speaking. Brainstorming. Mixing marriage and business. Colleagues with marital problems. Personality. Ambition. The 'special' therapist.

Chapter Thirteen   106
DIFFICULT PATIENTS
Palliative treatment. Steroids and strong medication. Repressed physical and emotional symptoms. The dangers of interfering with allopathic medication. Tranquilliser addiction: working with the patient's doctor. Abreactions. What not to treat when starting out. How to approach difficult treatments. Patients who ignore instructions and advice. Patient preferences. Men, women and sexual exploitation. False accusations. Transference, sexual or otherwise.

Chapter Fourteen   113
BURN OUT
How to avoid, deal with and recover from practitioner burn out. Long hours of listening to and dealing with physical, emotional and mental problems. Cut off points. Letting go. Workaholics. Responsibility weighs heavily. Hobbies. Patients' unreal expectations. Sabbaticals. Oversensitivity and how to deal with it. Hidden agendas and self scrutiny.

Chapter Fifteen   120
WORKING ON THE FRINGES
The Law of Opposites and the Law of Similars. Orthodox diagnosis and its uses. Conditions for which you cannot legally claim cure. Conditions which must be reported to the local authority. Conditions to be wary of. Cooperation between disciplines. Idealism and opening doors.

Chapter Sixteen   126
PREPARING FOR THE FUTURE
Property insurance. Accidental loss or damage cover. Unlimited indemnity. Public liability. Professional indemnity. Personal pension plans. Advantages of personal pension plans.

Chapter Seventeen   131
THE SINGLE EUROPEAN MARKET
Common Law and the Napoleonic Code. The Treaty of Rome. Exceptions to the rule and the Treaty of Paris. Vested interests of drug companies. Restrictions on herbs, homeopathic remedies, supplements and tonics etc. The importance of joining societies and organisations. Lobbying MPs and MEPs. Staying informed.

Chapter Eighteen   137
THE REWARDS

The value of natural medicine. Success is not always measured in money. The rewards of healing and helping others. Becoming part of humanity. Health and Gaia: the integration of people and planet. The personal support system. Philosophy of success. Pragmatism. Thinking big. Personal fulfilment and freedom for philanthropy. Moving into the future.

Appendix   142
PARTNERSHIP AGREEMENT:
An Example

DEDICATION

To the future of natural medicine
in all its rich variety and depth

ACKNOWLEDGEMENTS

The authors would like to thank Dr Jonathan Field, Sheilagh Richardson and Stephen Harrison for their valuable advice and constructive criticism.

We would like to thank Elizabeth Finn and Tim Harland for their dedication, support and contribution to this book. We would also like to acknowledge Ray Keedy and Richard Thomas for their contributions and thank William Crouch and Ivor Pead for their generosity and unstinted patience. Our thanks are also due to David Ford for the benefit of his creativity, flexibility and hard work.

Finally, we would like to thank Hayley without whom this book would never have been written.

FOREWORD
by
RICHARD THOMAS

The sociologists among you may have the answer but I don't: why is it that the most caring and hard-working people are often among the most disorganised? I do not know a bad practitioner, in the sense of a totally incompetent or corrupt practitioner, but I know an awful lot who are nowhere as effective as they could and should be simply because they seem to have little idea how to best organise themselves or their practice. The result, depressingly often, is a failed practice and a sick and worried practitioner. This is not because he or she is a poor healer (the very reverse is frequently the case) but simply because of an inability to understand the most basic requirements of administration.

It was for that reason we decided early on to start a regular column in the *Journal of Alternative and Complementary Medicine* on practice management. It was one of the earliest attempts that I know in this country to introduce practitioners, medical as well as non-medical, to the notion of effective management. Amazingly, the subject is hardly touched on at any of the many schools and colleges of natural medicine in Britain – many of them offering highly sophisticated courses in every other field of practice. Yet clearly it is a subject of crucial importance.

A practitioner who is not effective as a manager, whether of him or herself or others, is not going to be effective as a therapist. And to be effective as a manager means, whether we like it or not (and I'm one of those who doesn't much like it!), to be able to deal persuasively with the bank manager, punctually with the VAT returns and productively with the insurance broker. Effective management is as important as offering the right treatment to the right patient.

It seemed to be obvious, therefore, that if schools and colleges were going to teach practitioners how to treat and heal effectively they should also be teaching how to organise and run a practice effectively. My next brilliant idea was to put all this information into a book which we could then sell to all these deprived institutions! Sadly, like many of my best ideas, it came too late. Madeleine Harland and Glen Finn are, however, to be congratulated on producing a book which achieves exactly what I would have set out to achieve.

Being practitioners themselves they know very well the areas of greatest weakness and therefore the areas on which to concentrate attention. This they have done, in my opinion, both simply and intelligently. They treat the many, often complex, problems of running a practice with a directness and honesty which never fails to be highly practical. I am, above all, impressed with their positiveness – illustrated in the title.

Accounts and invoices are chores. But they have to be done, and done properly. If they are not, the practitioner not only suffers but the patient as well. For it is in financial mismanagement, or 'disease', that one can find the root cause for many a failed practitioner, failure which can prove terminal if not corrected. The authors have produced a book which is far more than simply a manual for running a business or even for running a business successfully. It is about running a business for the maximum health of both practitioner and patient. And if health does not equate with both success and happiness, I have yet to find what does.

Richard Thomas
Publisher and Editor-in-Chief
Journal of Alternative & Complementary Medicine

INTRODUCTION

Many talented practitioners qualify from their various colleges each year with a head full of knowledge, a heart full of good intentions and a score of worthy ideals to heal the sick. They then find that they are sadly lacking in business acumen. Business acumen is an essential ingredient which allows natural practitioners to work successfully in their field and to carry out what they have been trained to do. We know of many qualified people who have not managed to set up and succeed in practice. They are gifted healers but have a mental block when it comes to business. We also know of therapists who struggle to make ends meet or others that simply deserve to do better, given the time they have devoted to study and the hard work spent in setting up clinics. However laudable high ideals may seem, they can never put petrol in the car or dinner on the table unless they are supported by business management skills.

If you are one of those talented individuals who is a natural healer but shy of practice management, or if you just simply want to do better, this book is for you! It is written to demystify business management and logically explains all the various options for setting up clinics. In addition, it offers practical tested advice concerning accounts, VAT, business plans, employing staff and insurance cover and many other areas. Besides the nuts and bolts of financial planning and marketing, we explore the more subtle aspects of being successful, dealing with difficult situations that can arise at work and maintaining good health in what is a challenging career. Our aim is to condense our own experience in our respective practices and offer a practical guide to success, both in the business management field and on a more personal level.

Success is measured not only by the health of the bank balance but by quality of life as well. We consequently make no excuses for combining chapters on business skills with a more philosophical approach to being a natural medical practitioner. This is a unique and multi-dimensional career.

Our advice is simple and easy to follow. All it requires is motivation, a quality that most practitioners possess in abundance. After so much time devoted to study, often at our own expense, we owe it to ourselves, our families and our patients to offer the best. By being both competent and effective healers and running an efficient service, we fulfill a potential which benefits our patients and ourselves.

To embark upon a career in natural medicine is a fulfilling but demanding vocation. The world is full of sick people who need to be healed. It is a great ability to be able to relieve pain and suffering for one's fellow human being. Although the skills involved are many, this aspect is the relatively straightforward part, though we would never wish to imply that it is simple and without knowledge and art. What practitioners often find more difficult is the business management aspect of running clinics. Healing and financial acumen can appear to be in conflict with one another. We are so busy studying our various disciplines, passing exams and then putting our knowledge into practice, that there is little time to master the art of running a small business. Compared to the philosophy, techniques and practice of natural medicine, business skills often score a dull second.

Fortunately, business does not have to be dull. It is a game which we can play and should play to win. It can be filled with challenges, opportunities to solve problems *and* enjoyment. Business is also a very black and white area whilst natural medicine can often defy conventional explanation and definition and can be regarded as 'grey'. Consider your therapy as a large range of products and your business skills as a display in a shop window. Obviously, it is better that your window displays your products to the public to their greatest advantage. This is the purpose of being business-like in natural medicine, being able to offer your patients and clients the best service possible whilst also being secure and rewarded yourself. Success is a combination of having many happy clients and maintaining a good quality of life for yourself. After all, how can you heal others when you are beset by financial worries and ill health yourself? The equation simply does not add up.

Throughout this book we are attempting to bring together all the various forms of treatment under the same roof. Our book is not written to promote one therapy to the exclusion of another. Its purpose is to offer practical advice to practitioners, students and anyone considering a career in natural medicine on the business side of setting up and running a practice. We therefore use the word 'natural' with a certain amount of circumspection.

So often it is argued that the various therapies outside the orthodox medical science taught in our universities and teaching hospitals are 'alternative', 'fringe' or even 'complementary'. To some practitioners of certain disciplines, they are alternatives and can never be complementary. Orthodox medicine is regarded as such an anathema to long-term health that never the twain shall meet. To others, they remain complementary and can work side by side with orthodox approaches. Indeed, some branches of natural medicine are becoming accepted by the mainstream of orthodox medicine. It is not the intention of this book to divide up the branches of the tree and assess them as alternative or complementary. We are writing for the entire spectrum of therapies practised privately in the United Kingdom. Therefore, for the purpose of this book, we use the term 'natural' as a generic term meaning the therapies which harness the natural regenerative abilities inherent in all human beings, whether it be by tapping the vital force with homeopathic remedies or stimulating healing by using essential oils or pure manipulative techniques. By natural we mean healing without chemicalised, synthetic drugs.

We also take the liberty of referring to both practitioners and therapists, and patients and clients as the same. This is purely for ease of reference. In addition, the convention in the English language is to refer to the third person as a 'he'. For all the 'shes' out there, you are not forgotten. We merely wish to avoid a lengthy 'he and she' each time. There are times too when we use repetition to stress what we feel to be an essential point.

Finally, on a political note, we must also be aware that the single European Market will bring many changes to British trade and business practices. They do not currently bode well for natural practitioners. We must professionalise our services and join together to set standards in education, qualifications and practice. Business skills are an *essential* ingredient of this process. If we do not sharpen up our approach to natural medicine it is unlikely that all the therapies will survive and be available in 1992. Natural medicine contributes to the rich variety of our lives in Britain and we are very concerned that the choice the public currently has when seeking health care may be threatened in the future.

We trust you will find that this book fulfils its purpose and will help you on the road to business success and an improved quality of life.

Chapter 1

VOCATION VERSUS BUSINESS ACUMEN

Orthodox and natural medicine: uneasy bedfellows? Prevention rather than cure. Working outside the mainstream. A conflict between business and healing. The ethics and practice of charging fees.

Orthodox and Natural Medicine: Uneasy Bedfellows

Because natural medicine is not generally accepted and taught by the mainstream orthodox profession, natural practitioners often feel that they are swimming against the current of convention. They are aware that many of their qualifications remain unrecognised; that some people persist in alleging that a natural practitioner's skills are at best 'unproven' or at worst regarded as quackery. However learned and effective the therapist may be, he is still 'just a practitioner', overshadowed by the great god of orthodoxy.

We know that many of the conventions in the practice of medicine are historical and political. A great deal of what is prescribed in orthodox medicine lies in the hands of the drug companies who make a considerable amount of money from their wares and therefore wish to protect their industry. More simply, 'natural' cures and medicines are not promoted because they serve no commercial interest. But although there is this basic antagonism in philosophy and practice between natural and orthodox, we certainly do accept that the orthodox approach has its place in medicine.

We are not ostriches burying our heads in the sand. Natural medicine is not a viable option for everyone. Some people do not want it. Taking pills and putting the responsibility for our health on a respected individual is an easy way out in the short-term. Nor are we idealists. Natural medicine does not require expensive drugs but rather it takes time, an equally expensive resource. To change the system would require a revolution in our thinking and a complete change in our education. It is unlikely that such changes will come in the near future, even if those who direct the course of medicine wished it so. Without the support of the decision makers the likelihood of change is even more remote. The light at the end of the tunnel comes from the general public who increasingly use natural medicine and support the freedom to buy products and visit practitioners.

In this book we cite instances when conventional allopathic medicine plays an important role. We do recommend, however, that the natural therapies need to establish their position as the *first* line of treatment and not the last. Very often we see patients who have had strong suppressive medication, or even surgery. They finally arrive at our clinics, often in desperation and as a last resort. This emphasis needs to change. We must educate people to seek the natural approaches first. Then, if necessary, they can explore more radical measures. To make this ideal a reality, for the sake of our own particular therapy, our individual practices need to reflect a professional approach, whether it is glossy and 'hi-tech' or relaxed and informal. We are not suggesting that we imitate orthodox doctors in their style of work but that we offer the very best services within our area of expertise.

Prevention Rather Than Cure

The philosophy of most of the natural therapies is to be preventative. This is something we have grown to appreciate over many years of practice. The orthodox system of diagnosis approaches health quite differently; that before any medication can be prescribed, the complaint or condition must already be quite well established. The diagnosis must precede the medication. In contrast, the natural approach can administer treatment based on the presenting symptoms at a very early stage of development before they have developed into a classifiable, full-blown 'disease'. This enables the body's own healing system to correct the imbalance in good time before an allopathic diagnosis is possible and, more importantly, before the destructive process of disease has taken hold.

Even in the 'mental' rather than physical area of healing, it would be so much easier to treat a client with a fairly simple form of stress management or bereavement counselling rather than wait until these life crises have compounded themselves by further difficulties and caused a full blown nervous disease.

An example of the pragmatics of prevention rather than cure would be the analogy of a house with a leaking roof. The orthodox system would seek to collect the droplets in buckets and pans. After a while, the buckets would need to be emptied. The rain would still be leaking in whilst the occupier of the house was emptying the pans and buckets. The preventative measure necessary is for the person to get up on the roof and fix it, to stop the leak. If they are wise, able and have the materials, they would repair the leak long before it became a gaping hole and the rainy season started. They would choose the first opportunity and make good the roof. They would not wait for a storm to brew, for the wind to lash at the hole effecting further damage, and for torrents of rain to pour into the house. The repair work would be kept to a minimum and quickly finished. This is the ideal of prevention which has long been argued by so called 'health fanatics' who claimed that the food we ate and the exercise we took directly affected our well-being. What was once a controversial subject is now common currency.

To treat the cause and not the effect is a simple philosophy but it has true depth and worth in its meaning. Every human being should have the choice of all the possible approaches, orthodox and otherwise, at their disposal in times of need and illness. But long-term solutions can only be gained by adopting the preventative aspect. Nature forces upon us many lessons. On a world scale, we continue to over-chemicalise and deplete both the regenerative and non-regenerative resources of the very earth we depend upon and suffer the side effects of pollution and other imbalances with such actions.

The same is happening in our own bodies. We know that certain drugs are iatrogenic and that they actually cause disease in the long term. Their curative properties are only suppressing symptoms which gather energy and rise up later on as more severe and more chronic illnesses. Even if a drug is not iatrogenic, it may have unpleasant side effects which reduce the quality of the patient's life. This process is a mirror to our farming methods. We feed offal to our herbivores which then develop degenerative diseases. We farm intensively, spraying crops to increase yields. The chemicals leach into our soil and water table causing pollution, effecting wildlife habitats and domestic animals. Our environment is impoverished and ultimately those chemicals find their way into our food and water. Salmonella and mad cow disease develop. Excessive nitrates and nitrites affect our water. Silage pollutes the rivers and kills fish. The land becomes a cocktail of the residues of fertilisers, weed killers and insecticides. The results unfold around us. Do we really understand the effects?

Working Outside The Mainstream

Although natural practitioners may still be swimming against the tide of convention in the majority of teaching hospitals, the public are gradually accepting the various disciplines and philosophies and are actively seeking them out. Even though the National Health Service rarely offers natural medicine to its patients, the public are prepared to go outside the pre-paid health care system and pay again. Increasingly, practitioners are being freed from the burden of feeling that they must imitate doctors to gain credence from patients. They are accepted as professionals in a very different system of health care and they are no longer made to feel unqualified or 'second class' as healers by the media. Accusations of quackery are fading as the curative effects of natural medicine become a more common currency.

In some isolated situations practitioners are working alongside GPs and specialists. Our world is changing. It is not by any means a rosy picture. The politics of orthodoxy continues to threaten natural medicine yet, in the same breath, public enthusiasm for natural medicine is growing and promoting the cause. Practitioners are no longer voices crying in the wilderness.

The natural medicine colleges in the UK are growing in number and increasing in size. More and more people are considering a career as a practitioner. They are drawn towards the various professions and feel they have a 'vocation'. At the same time, many disciplines are beginning to meet together and agree on basic qualifications. We hope that this is a beginning and that the various branches of natural medicine will link together and form a powerful tree, deeply rooted in a common goal of professional excellence and the freedom to practise long into the future.

Conflict Between Business and Healing

Because the work load of training courses is demanding and is often carried out by students financing their own studies by full-time jobs, there has been little room in the curriculum for learning business skills. Many of the colleges in the country have, until recently, given little attention to the subjects of practice management and setting up a clinic.

One of the aims of this book is to familiarise the student or working practitioner with the many options that are available to him, with detailed information presented in an accessible, understandable form on business and personal management. We have no wish to indulge in 'business speak' or present a stodgy manual for practice management. Drawing upon our own hard-earned experience, and that of fellow colleagues, we hope this book imparts as much information as possible, enabling the budding student to prepare for the many pitfalls that could arise. He will then be forewarned and able to side-step some of the obvious and not so obvious mistakes that could occur.

This book is also for the practitioner who is already seeing patients but wishes to expand and consider new options. To this end, the subjects covered are of equal relevance to experienced and fledgling therapists alike. It is so common to find very gifted people-orientated practitioners who care little for practice management and 'success' in its crude material form.

Of course, a gift for healing will substantially sustain a therapist at work and will ensure a good reputation from word of mouth, created by grateful patients.

Business acumen is never a substitute for a genuine healing ability and care. However, the healing arts do not negotiate contracts, set up accounts, enlist accountants and sign leases. They do not deal with the Inland Revenue and the VAT man! This material side is the workhorse or framework of the practice. So often ignored, it can become the nightmare. Despite being gifted, therapists do give up their work because they simply cannot pay the bills. This is tragic for their own self-development and for the public at large. The best practitioners often make the worst business people and people with a talent for business are not necessarily very good practitioners. We hope therefore to address this problem for students and practising therapists alike.

The Ethics and Practice of Charging Fees

Believe it or not, one of the biggest stumbling blocks is actually charging the patient. In the practice of natural medicine we come into such close contact with our patients. We are not afraid to draw out and release very deep-rooted fears and secrets, to come out from behind the desk and touch our patients. We hear all about marital, parental or financial problems and, at the end of a consultation, we develop such a good rapport with the patient that he feels the therapist is a friend. Then we have to revert back to the businessman's role and charge the fee for our time. How can we justify this when we are here to help the sick?

For National Health doctors the problem is solved by a fixed system of financial rewards and support of an established network of surgeries and hospitals, although this could change as new NHS legislation develops. For the private therapist, it is a very different story. There is no established network. He often finds himself with a diploma in hand and boundless enthusiasm but with precious little business experience. He must then make provision to practise his art and live off the proceeds in a highly competitive and expensive world.

Not only are patients in this country unused to parting with actual cash for medical treatment but healing has always adopted spiritual overtones. It is often regarded as a God-given ability and therefore should be free. One might ask, "Aren't we adding to our poor patient's burden by asking for a fee?"

We advise you to think carefully about this specific question as a student. If you feel that you will have any problems in charging a fee then seek practical advice from one of your experienced colleagues. Also talk to an accountant. This is one of the most important steps before embarking on a business. Find out what your colleagues are charging in your area, set your own fees in relation to them and then outline your plans to your accountant. Ask him if yours is a realistic figure to charge and will enable you to survive. This also helps psychologically. You can mentally lay the blame for the fee at his door every time you charge a patient!

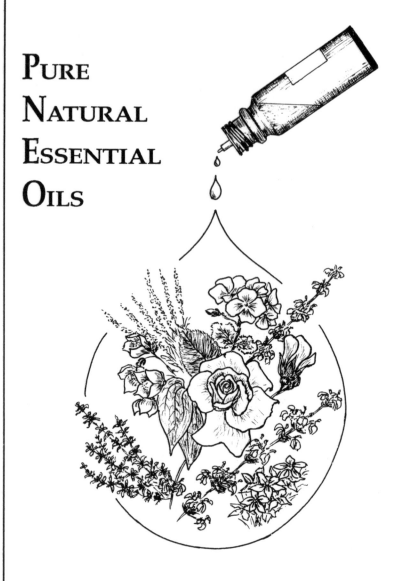

PURE
NATURAL
ESSENTIAL
OILS

Quality Essential Oils, Vegetable Oils and Absolutes,
Floral Waters, Books and Bottles

Very Competitive Prices

Discounts available for Practitioners

Guaranteed 48 hour mail order services

ESSENTIALLY OILS LIMITED

Coventry Trading Estate, Baginton, Coventry, Warwickshire CV3 4FJ
Tel: 0203 639074.   Fax: 0203 639280

Your fees should be reviewed annually. You may decide on a rate for OAPs, students and children (we discuss this in more detail later). This rate should not then be altered for anyone (unless, when you are experienced, you recognise a genuine case of hard luck). Once you can justify altering for one, you will soon find yourself on the slippery slope of rarely charging the correct fee and your accountant will be none too pleased. Remember the golden rule: if at the end of each month you cannot meet your commitments like rent, mortgage, food, petrol, remedies, stationery etc. then how can you continue to practise your vocation? Business acumen enables the continuing pleasure of fulfilling the vocation to heal. It is not in conflict with it.

In an ideal world, we would not have to worry about accounts, bills, fees and marketing. The therapist would happily ply his trade, secure in the knowledge that healing was an end in itself. This vision is what many of us would like to believe and the cut and thrust of business can come as an unpleasant surprise.

Some practitioners have even been tarred with the brush of being too canny, too 'commercial'. Their colleagues have looked down on them for being too concerned with efficient accounting. We know of a clinic which installed a wordprocessor in the days when they were relatively uncommon. This innovation was met with suspicion. Why should technology be in conflict with natural healing? If it makes our life easier and our service more efficient, surely it is a good thing? Natural medicine is linked with the future and not trapped by the past.

Certainly, we would not wish to convey to our readers that we are 'only in it for the money'. This book expresses a genuine desire to help the healer establish a degree of business acumen and to be 'street wise'. 'Forewarned is forearmed.' In this world, the armour of good business skills is essential and when we set up in practice we must realise that we are also in business.

If we as practitioners are to heal and be successful in our professional lives it is essential for us to have a high quality of life ourselves. This means having as few worries as possible. Gather a good team about you. Find an accountant, a solicitor, a bank account manager and a bank business manager and make sure they are people who you can trust and that you can ring them for advice when you need it. If we are to be justified in charging for our services, then we are by definition professional and we must act in a professional manner.

Neither must we be afraid of paying professional advisors for their help and experience if necessary. A piece of professional advice that has to be paid for may have a hundred-fold return where advice with no cost placed on it may ultimately have little or no return. Do not forget though, that as with any advice, it is up to you whether or not you take it. Other people's opinions should certainly be listened to, but they should never replace the importance of your own judgement and understanding. Also, be aware that your team must be a good one. Not all so called 'professionals' are perfect and they can make errors. Be astute and realistic when appointing the team and research them well. The best recommendations are personal. We always work with people who have been recommended by colleagues we respect and who have a proven track record. We also choose people who are interested in us and our projects and who will assure us of a personal and efficient service.

In this book we cover an array of subjects from basic practicalities, the nuts and bolts, such as working from home, renting space, buying leases and freehold properties, to marketing your services, accounting and the implications of the single European Market. There are also less tangible considerations like the inspiration behind our choice of career, maintaining harmonious business relationships between colleagues, practitioner 'burn out', difficult patients, and even the more 'esoteric' psychology of success.

Practice management, at first glance, would seem to be a dry and boring subject. We hope we will change that and demonstrate that it is all about learning how systems and people tick and about being positive, realistic, flexible and open to challenges. There is always a great satisfaction in doing anything well. We aim to make the path to success more fulfilling and easier for our readers to tread. So let's start walking . . .

Chapter 2

WORKING FROM HOME

THE ADVANTAGES:
Inexpensive option which is intimate, relaxed and homely. Your partner can act as receptionist.
THE DISADVANTAGES:
Setting up the room. Family. Animals. Amateur image. Security and theft. Accusations of assault. Obscene and threatening telephone calls. Privacy.
OTHER CONSIDERATIONS:
What you need to work from home. Telephone. Answer phone. Waiting room. Overheads. 'Change of use'. Capital gains tax.

When starting a practice, there are a number of options to choose from in relation to where you want to work. The most obvious choice is to set up a clinic in a room in your own home. This decision can have many positive aspects to it. It can also have some disadvantages. We will explore both aspects to help you reach your own conclusions. You may already run a successful practice in a clinic away from your home and wish to expand or you may be fresh from college and starting up. Whatever your circumstances, here are some points to consider.

The Advantages

Using a room or rooms in your own home is inexpensive. You do not have to consider paying rent which may be subject to yearly or half yearly increases. You do not have to borrow money to buy a suitable property. Whatever money you earn in fees is yours to keep as income. There are no hidden charges, no bombshells on maintenance costs, or bills to be shared with other practitioners. What is yours stays yours and goes directly into your business account to draw on as wages, capital items and expenses.

Being at home can also engender the kind of atmosphere which you require in your style of practice. It is intimate and personal. You can't help that. Your personality and idiosyncracies are stamped upon the place. This can work to your advantage. The intimate and homely feel to the place can relax your client or patient and your first meeting together may be easier, being based in your home, albeit in a designated room of your choice. The interview can be conducted with less tension. Unlike a formal interview, this consultation can be made to feel on more trusting and friendly terms. The patient will sense this and be able to open up and express feelings more willingly. If your practice has an emphasis on discussing emotional and mental symptoms rather than on the physical problem of the patient or client, you will find that you elicit information more easily. Being relaxed, your patient will begin to drop his mask more readily and allow you to approach difficult subjects with greater assurance. There is often more humour in these circumstances because the patient is relaxed and able to laugh at his problems. Certainly, for all natural therapists, this is a very useful tool in the process of treatment.

Home also offers a quiet privacy that is impossible to find in a busy clinic. Some patients are embarrassed about 'alternative' therapies and do not wish to feel they are announcing that they have a problem to the world by walking through a clinic door. They do not want people to know that they need treatment and may worry about being seen visiting a practitioner in a busy town. Your home is a protective environment and a sometimes necessary secret for them in an otherwise intrusive world. The occasion also arises when a patient's partner does not approve of the chosen form or course of treatment. They may think it is bunkum or too expensive. Your home offers the patient a place to visit out of the critical eyes of friends or relatives.

This aspect of privacy and quiet can be a great advantage. There is nothing worse than teaching relaxation or hypnotising someone close to a busy street with doors slamming and juggernauts pounding down the road! There is also nothing worse than being disturbed by the telephone or a knock on your door when you are discussing a particularly personal and painful problem or entering a client into a deep trance state. In an instant, all your hard work and efforts to create an atmosphere of calm and trust are shattered by the peel of a bell or a loud clatter. Valuable therapeutic moments can be lost.

For instance, an acupuncturist friend was once listening intently to a young woman as she related a particularly harrowing time in her childhood. She had not disclosed any of this in the two previous appointments and the acupuncturist was so pleased that she felt able at last to reveal these details to her. It was about 6 p.m. on a dark winter's evening. The other practitioners at the clinic had left for home and so had the receptionist. The acupuncturist's attention was suddenly taken from her patient as her ears caught the sound of the front door opening. Perhaps someone had forgotten something or perhaps the wind had blown the door ajar as it was apt to do occasionally? She heard no footsteps and turned her full attention back to her patient. In the next moment the acupuncturist heard a definite noise in reception and could restrain her curiosity no longer. She gently extricated her attention from her patient and excused herself, leaving the room to investigate. She discovered a youth of about twelve standing in reception asking to use the toilet. She was rather taken aback by this request but he said he had been to the clinic with his mother. Being a trusting sort, she believed him and led him downstairs to the toilet. As they turned at the bottom of the stairs, the youth shot out of the door and into the night. The acupuncturist returned perplexed to reception where she found the petty cash box opened but luckily nothing had been taken. She was then left to explain her absence to the waiting patient and recapture the lost rapport.

It was another valuable lesson for the practitioner. Apart from the inconvenience of being interrupted at work, for more serious security reasons, never leave your front door off the latch if you are alone in the building. Never leave the reception area unattended and the desk unlocked, even for a moment. You never know who is sitting in reception taking note of monetary transactions and the movements of the practitioner(s). That young lad had cased the acupuncturist's clinic very well. You are equally vulnerable at home. But more of security measures later . . .

On a practical level when working from home, you may have a spouse or a friend living with you who can also assist you at work without having to go anywhere or neglect other tasks he or she may have to perform. He can answer the phone for you while you are in consultation, receive patients at the door and settle them down while they wait. He can book appointments and deal with the financial side of the treatment if you wish to separate the process of payment from the consultation itself. In all he is a free receptionist on hand when you need him but able to get on with other pursuits and tasks when it is quiet. This is extremely useful as receptionists are expensive and sometimes under-occupied in the beginning of a practice when clients' attendances are erratic and there are lulls in the appointments.

The Disadvantages

If the room or rooms are easily converted to a clinic or consulting room, you can get out your paint brush, acquire the necessary equipment and set to work creating the environment of your choice. But what do you need to start up a clinic and how should you lay out the room and organise your house for your business without affecting the lives of those you live with?

Obviously, the first consideration is the room you will use to see patients in, store records and generally use as an office. The ideal is to choose a room on the ground floor which then prevents patients from having to climb the stairs. They may have a disability which makes stairs impossible. They will also not enter the most private area of your family's life - the bedrooms, unmade beds, yesterday's socks, your children's grubby sports gear can remain in glorious disarray upstairs whilst you practise your skills in the tidy calm of your clinic. Your patients are none the wiser! However, this arrangement does presuppose that you have a lavatory on the ground floor.

Assuming that you have the space, where will you work at home? For some practitioners the living room is a reasonable choice. All they may need is a place to hold a consultation. They are comfortable with an informal and personal atmosphere. The disadvantages to this are the very personal nature of the room and the fact that this room has to be out of bounds to the rest of the household in working hours. This may suit a working household but will be impractical if you have children.

You also have to consider the noise problem when working from home. Children coming in from a day at school and animals all contribute to it. If you have a dog he may bark when another patient comes to the door. He may also need to be restrained. Dog or cat hairs will find their way into the room, on to the furniture and your patients' clothes, not to mention the problems of contravening the clean surface rules for acupuncturists!

It is not unknown for patients to be allergic to animal hairs. An aromatherapist once had a patient who was allergic to cats. The patient spent the entire consultation sneezing and did not return! Another time she received a patient at her door who had been attacked by a black dog in childhood. The patient had a very real terror of dogs, especially black ones. The therapist happened to have a black male labrador. The patient could not be treated at the home and had to go to the therapist's clinic. Allergy to natural gas is also not uncommon. Be prepared for these difficulties.

Animals can cause many problems and add to the sloppy amateurish image that working from home can engender if your clinic room is on top of the family but they can also be of help. The aromatherapist was a single woman alone and working from home. The large black dog was a comfort and a deterrent. One of her patients was a detective inspector. He always expressed concern that she used her home for work. He felt it exposed her to unnecessary risks. It would be so easy for a man posing as a patient to rape and/or rob her. For this reason the therapist never treated men alone at home. She made sure someone else was about. Luckily, she did have other clinics to go to as well as adults sharing the household. She could place clients away from home or make sure someone else was in the house.

If you only work from home and are on your own in the day you open yourself up to the public. Strangers come into your home. They may choose to help themselves to your property whilst you are with another patient. They may

misuse your telephone. They may steal your cashbox. They may assault you or even accuse you of assault. All these possibilities have occurred. The problems of security must be very carefully thought out if you are considering working from home.

Being alone with a patient is a risk from a psychological and legal point of view. Should any disagreement occur it is always your word against their's. Male GPs and registrars rarely if ever examine women without the presence of a nurse as a witness. You, as a practitioner, must consider that you are vulnerable. You do not know your patient or his history. He may accuse you of assault or attempt to assault you. You may be accused of unethical behaviour even though you are entirely professional. An experienced GP who practiced hypnotherapy used to have a note on his desk saying that all conversations within the treatment room were being recorded for the protection of both the patient and the doctor. Not all consultations were necessarily recorded, of course, but the technique worked none the less.

We are not asking you to suspect that every patient is a potential criminal, hysteric or neurotic. We are only asking you to consider carefully the implications of being alone with people in intimate circumstances, particularly if you examine, manipulate or hypnotise them. You are vulnerable if your patient's consent to treatment is only implied or verbal in the eyes of the law. A competent and successful chiropractor of our acquaintance is particularly careful when treating minors under 16 years old. He makes sure the patient's parent or guardian sign a form to allow him to examine the child. Then he requires that the adult responsible sign another form consenting to treatment. If consent is only informal or implied it will not protect a practitioner in court. It is always better to obtain written consent to treatment. This will give you a degree of security but it will not protect you from allegations or, needless to say, if you do actually assault your patient! There have been several recent instances of practitioners being charged with assault and this is therefore a very important consideration. You cannot afford to be idealistic about people.

Besides the problems of assault, burglary is growing in epidemic proportions in our society. Here are some suggestions to avoid tempting thieves. According to police records a professional thief spends approximately three minutes committing his crime. Therefore make your house as unattractive as possible:
1) Maintain a low profile. Do not leave valuable items and cash conspicuously lying around.
2) Bright lights, open spaces, fences and walls discourage unwanted entry.
3) Install evidence of a good alarm system (even if you haven't one!).
4) Leave music playing or the television on when you go out.
5) Buy a time switch and set it to turn on in the evenings whilst you are on holiday or out. They are inexpensive.

6) Have a secret place to store your takings which is not obvious to a burglar, i.e. a cash box built into the wall behind a dummy plug socket or behind a picture. Bank your fees as often as you can.

7) Ask your local crime prevention officer for advice. He is an expert and there to help you.

8) Join or set up Neighbourhood Watch. For a minimal amount of time and the price of a sign you do not create a vigilante group but rather a safer environment where neighbours keep an eye on each others' property whilst the owners are out or away.

We are not paranoid. Burglary is the fastest growing crime in Britain. If you run a business from a property which takes cash as a matter of course you invite the possibility of being robbed. It is a sad indictment on our society, but true.

Aside from physical abuse and robbery there is always verbal abuse to consider! Your home telephone number becomes public property. A lady therapist we know received obscene phone calls which were unpleasant and frightening. It was hard to gauge how harmless they were. There was always the possibility that the caller would carry out his threats.

There are various ways of approaching this problem. British Telecom advise that you hang up immediately but gently. Never give your name and address and contact the police if the calls continue. Your local BT customer service manager offers advice on this problem but reports indicate that neither the police or BT are much help. BT will intercept all calls free to your number but only for a limited period of time. You can always use an answer phone to vet calls and then return calls when required. If the situation becomes intolerable, the other option is to change your number but this costs money and is inconvenient. It means changing your stationery and contacting all your clients as well as paying BT for a new number. You may lose valuable contacts. Nuisance calls are against the law and distressing but they are rarely more than a nuisance. We advise tolerance and patience. If the receiver of the call displays minimal reaction the caller will go elsewhere.

In addition, the home phone number makes you vulnerable day and night to patients calling. This may seem good in theory. You can respond to emergencies and offer your patients a complete service. Unfortunately, you are never off duty. You can be reached at any time day or night. You can feel that you are losing control of your life. Your home, which used to be a place in which to relax and find sanctuary, becomes a 24 hour office. You could start to dread answering the phone. A female counsellor was once treating a woman with a violent husband. He telephoned the counsellor on the day she returned from her honeymoon with a string of inaccurate accusations as to what she had told his wife in a consultation. It was not the best way to end the holiday!

This problem of a loss of privacy is fundamental when working from home. You can buy an answer phone and have completely separate rooms but it is still your home. For some practitioners this does not present a problem, but for others it can be very stressful. It does need careful thought. It is important to decide what kind of person you are. Is your life your work and can you cope with the stress of being on call 24 hours a day or do you need to escape? You may have a busy family life with responsibilities to others as well as your clients. You may have minimal social and family commitments and be unaffected by business calls at anti-social times. Only you can assess your individual circumstances. Do that honestly and with consideration for your personal responsibilities and then you are likely to find a balance.

Other Considerations

Problems aside, what do you need to work from home? Firstly, you need a room to work in. As mentioned before, this could be your living room but most practitioners have a separate room to work from. Depending on your discipline, you may need a couch or bench, a screen for your patients to change behind; chairs, a desk, a telephone. If you are an acupuncturist you are legally required to have a wash basin in the room in which you work. Some require a minimum pile on the carpet, wash basins, tiles one third of the way up the wall in the consulting room. You must check with your health authority for specifications. Should certain demands be inconsiderate or awkward to fulfil, your professional society will provide you with support and advice in individual cases.

You may favour a room with an air of informality which does not resemble an office or a clinic. On the other hand you may need a spotless and formal environment to work in. Whatever your preference, it is essential that you have somewhere where you can store your patients' notes safely and away from curious eyes and keep your bills and papers. A desk and a filing cabinet are essential for your organisation.

A telephone is a necessity. A useful addition is the often dreaded answer phone. It means you can go out and never miss vital messages. You can also turn it on when you are deep in consultation, if you are alone in the house, and when there is no one else to take your calls. There is nothing more off-putting than a shrill and relentless telephone demanding attention, but calls left unanswered may be a lost potential appointment. The answer phone gives you choice and more control. You can choose who and when to phone back. You can choose to be out when you are in or in when you are out! Nevertheless, for reasons already stated, we recommend that you are never alone in your clinic with patients.

Another alternative to maintain privacy would be to have another telephone installed in your office using a different number on another line. This could be used solely for your practice, answered only during business hours and with an answer phone taking calls after hours. Your patients then need never know your other private number. As well as allowing you more privacy, this system will possibly even be considered more professional by your patients than answering the phone at all hours. The disadvantage, of course, is the not inconsiderable expense of installing and renting another telephone line, but remember that it is tax deductible.

Another consideration is what to do with your waiting patients. You may want to put them in your living room if it is available but not if you have valuable items on display. You may have room for seating in the hallway. Whatever the case, you must have somewhere for them. They can't wait outside! People are not often on time. They are either very early or very late and few practitioners are able to clock-watch. Our experience is that many run over time. There will almost certainly be times when one or more people are waiting. What will you do with these bodies? It is always good to provide reading material and a comfortable seat at least. Be prepared to have your house scrutinised minutely. The practitioner is a fascinating animal to his patient, especially when at home in his lair.

Although we said that working from home was inexpensive, there are overheads to consider. Decorating costs, furniture, office equipment, higher telephone bills, the purchase of an answer phone and extra heating and lighting costs must be covered. Do not be too optimistic in your budgeting.

If you as the householder are the only practitioner, then your house remains as a solely domestic building if you only use less than 10% of the total area of the property. If you either let your room to another practitioner or employ someone (other than those living in the house), then you are liable to apply to the local council for a 'change of use'. (*See Chapter 6* for details on the procedure.)

Finally, there is the potential problem of capital gains tax. If you use one room exclusively in your house for business but charge all or most of the household bills to the business, you risk incurring capital gains tax when you sell the property. This means that 60% of the profit on the house can be taken in tax. The way to avoid this is to charge a 'management fee' to the business for the use of heating and lighting. Ask your accountant exactly how much this should be. It depends on how much you use your home for business. Many people have been caught out by small mistakes which have potentially catastrophic results. It is always worth checking in great detail.

A more serious consideration is the position regarding the Uniform Business Rate which is distinct from the Community Charge. As we all know, the Community Charge is assessed on individuals regardless of where they live and how they conduct their business. The uniform business rate is separate and possibly of greater concern. The Local District Valuer is responsible for assessing the rateable value of business premises. If a business sets aside for exclusive use part of a private residence, the District Valuer is entitled to assess that part of the residence for the uniform business rate. The procedure is that the value of the part of the property used would be given a rateable value, in line with its current market rental value, and the uniform business rate of approximately 34 pence in the pound would apply.

Where a room or area is not exclusively used for business, the Inland Revenue would not look to assess for uniform business rate. Where a substantial amount of business is carried out from a private residence but an argument is put up that part of the residence is not set aside exclusively, the District Valuer looks at other evidence that a business is being carried out. This would include separate telephone lines for business use and the amount of comings and goings of clients, suppliers etc.

Simply, for the practitioner, make your clinic the household library and study or some other such appropriate function. Keep a low profile and practise happily without antagonising your neighbours.

Working from home can be very pleasurable and profitable. Many practitioners run successful and happy clinics this way. They are organised and they have considered the positive and negative sides of the coin. Your patients are individuals. Some will like coming to your house, others will be put off by it. Therefore, the best option is to have a clinic in the house and another or others elsewhere. This leads us on to the advantages and disadvantages of renting time in a clinic.

Chapter 3

RENTING TIME IN A CLINIC

THE ADVANTAGES:
Low overheads. Renting the time you need. Building up slowly. Referrals to and from other practitioners. Support and professional stimulation from other practitioners. Not being isolated. Self doubt and confidence. Clinical and professional atmosphere. Credibility of working with other established practitioners. Reputation (good and bad) by association. Image. Goodwill of established therapists. Buffer between you and you patients.

THE DISADVANTAGES:
No control over rent increases. Contractual obligations. Limited say on decoration and room layout etc. Personality and professional differences with other practitioners.

OTHER CONSIDERATIONS:
As patients build up you may run out of time and space. A note to fledgling practitioners.

Perhaps you are unable to work from your home or you want to expand your practice into another geographical area? An alternative option to working from your house is to rent half a day or more in a clinic, doctor's surgery or natural health centre which is already well established. It could equally be above a shop or even in a residential home for elderly people, a possibility we know has been used with success. Any of these options can be a very good way of building up a practice and becoming known in your community.

The Advantages

Your overheads will be lower than renting an office full time and establishing your own clinic from new. You will pay only for the time you rent and you can gauge the time you will usefully need to practise your skills so that you are always busy seeing people when you are there. You may wish to rent a morning or afternoon and then extend your time if you can when you become busier.

Another option which may be negotiable for the fledgling practitioner is to pay a minimal rent and then pay a percentage of the fees you take at the clinic to the clinic manager. This way you do not find yourself paying so much rent in slack times. This is a good system but it is often hard to come by as the clinic does not benefit so much from your time spent there. It may be negotiable in the early days on a trial period while you are finding your feet but will revert to the usual system of rent in relation to time taken after a couple of months. With time you will become too busy for this system to remain feasible in any case, being run off your feet with patients and therefore awash with fees!

A figure that has been offered to new practitioners joining an established clinic was 20% of their fees taken in the clinic. This was a generous arrangement. A higher percentage would be more realistic. Obviously, as soon as the practitioner becomes successful he can't wait to get off the percentage arrangement as it is no longer in his interest to do this.

Renting in a clinic will have some overheads. Sometimes a fee is asked on joining the group; this may cover changing the clinic advertising to include you and your therapy, replacing furniture, plants and other renewable extras. You may be asked to contribute to the equipping of the room from scratch if the clinic is starting up. You may have to pay a percentage of the telephone, heating and lighting bills according to the time you spend there. You may be asked to contribute to the receptionist's wages. If there is no receptionist you may have to fill in at reception for other practitioners as they will for you on a reciprocal arrangement. You may also have to answer calls for other practitioners whilst in consultation yourself. These aspects must be clear at the onset of your agreement to avoid misunderstandings and bad feelings.

Besides not having the burden of a full time clinic at a delicate time in your practising life, there are other advantages to renting space in an established clinic. Because you only rent the time you need you can build up your patient list slowly. This is less stressful. You are not worrying about money as the clock ticks by or taking on more than you can cope with in the early stages of practice. You can take the clients you know will benefit from your skills and refer on those who are out of your depth. Your confidence can be built upon slowly and financial pressure will not solely dictate the reason for treating all and sundry.

Obviously, there are times in every practitioner's life when they simply cannot treat a particular person. This may be due to a critical lack of experience or an inharmonious meeting of personalities. Whatever the reason, it is better to bow to it than to press on regardless with one eye on the rent cheque. Of course, inexperience is not always a reason for shying away from cases otherwise no one would gain experience in the first place! It is necessary at times to decline gracefully however, when a practitioner feels he is out of his depth. The advice and support of trusted and respected colleagues is invaluable at these times.

There are times when the discipline that one practitioner follows is clearly not helping the patient. The treatment appears to have come to a dead end.

Sometimes the patient does not respond to a particular therapy or has reached a plateau in the progress of his treatment. Often a change of practitioner or therapy is the way forward.

We have seen someone benefit hugely from acupuncture but respond minimally to homeopathy. This was no reflection on the skills of the practitioner but an expression of that patient's individuality. It is very difficult to assess whether your treatment is incorrect or that the therapy has run its course. It is equally difficult to tell the patient that he needs to seek help elsewhere but usually that patient is aware that he is no longer making progress. If the emotional and physical symptoms get worse and do not respond to your treatment over a period of time, it is appropriate to discuss the lack of progress with the patient and review alternative forms of treatment if possible. This is by no means an admission of failure or defeat, but perhaps an acknowledgement that the patient/practitioner relationship has become too comfortable and cosy: a stalemate. A change to this may be the catalyst to move the patient forward again.

There are also instances of two skills combining for the better. A patient may come in with a physical problem and may benefit from relaxation therapy or counselling from a psychotherapist. Alternatively, a hypnotherapist may enlist the help of a chiropractor or aromatherapist in helping a client to regain his health fully. Working in a shared clinic with colleagues from other disciplines gives one the flexibilty to refer patients 'in house'.

Working in a clinic can offer you a support system from other practitioners. This can be very useful. In college there is always someone to discuss cases with and courses of treatment. When the practitioner leaves, he or she can often find they are isolated. The interchange of ideas and experience is very useful and stimulating. It is also a great confidence builder.

It is certain that every practitioner experiences self-doubt at some stage or another. Having peers to talk to and exchange advice with is a great help. The view of an experienced therapist, whatever the discipline, can be invaluable. We have certainly benefited from the experience and counsel of fellow practitioners over the years and cannot overemphasize the value of their friendship and support.

In addition to having a support system from other practitioners, there is another advantage to working with other professionals in a clinic. It is one of image and credibility. Just as one can appear amateur at home, a clinical environment lends a sense of professionalism and having other colleagues can bolster this view in the eyes of the public. This can sometimes be infuriating to the older established therapist who has studied long and worked from home for years who is compared unfavourably to a young inexperienced therapist who

Make a note of the 1991 dates

The Health Show
4–7 July 1991 · OLYMPIA · LONDON

The Health Show at London's prestigious Olympia 2 Exhibition Hall is the largest public health and fitness show in the U.K.

Special feature areas cover natural therapies, healthy eating, fitness, organic growing and green living.

One entire floor is devoted to natural therapies and includes a demonstration stage and a Practitioners Lounge.

Further details from the organisers, Swan House Special Events Ltd

LONDON
TOURIST BOARD AND
CONVENTION BUREAU
MEMBER

Swan House Special Events Ltd.

Holly Road, Hampton Hill, Middlesex TW12 1PZ
Tel No. 081 783 0055   Fax No. 081 783 1678

Member
aeo
Association of
Exhibition Organisers

suddenly sets up in a plush clinic in the same town. The less experienced person can *appear* more professional and more informed. It is maddening but true that one's capabilities are often assessed by the public on appearance rather than reality. Fortunately, word of mouth is probably a more valuable source of recommendation than the environment one chooses to work in. However, image is a consideration. Clinics do help a natural practitioner in the battle to become accepted by the general public who perhaps still have a tendency to see 'fringe' medicine as quackery, although this old fashioned view is on the way out.

By renting space in an established clinic, one also 'buys' the goodwill of the other practitioners working there. It is a question of reputation by association. When working on one's own, one is relying solely on oneself to create a good name in the 'business'. The most effective way is invariably word of mouth. Working with others can enhance one's reputation. If you share space you also share good or bad reputations so make sure the clinic which you are contemplating working from is well regarded in the community. Negative gossip can be very hard to overcome and may affect your ability to gain a good patient list. On the other hand, working with reputable well established practitioners will enhance your reputation by virtue of your association with them. It is a great boost. They may even refer patients to you.

You may find that GPs in your area are open-minded about complementary medicine and are happy to rent you space in their surgeries. Medical doctors practising homeopathy or acupuncture privately, use this system. It is also possible for practitioners like hypnotherapists, chiropractors, osteopaths and chiropodists to work hand in hand with sympathetic GPs. If you do not actually work under the same roof, you may find GPs are willing to recommend your services to their patients, especially when the problem is more 'mental' than 'physical'. We know a GP who regularly refers patients to a professional homeopath and a hypnotherapist, a mutually beneficial arrangement for all concerned.

The clinic is also a great buffer between you and your work. You can choose not to be contacted outside working hours. No more late night phone calls from patients requiring treatment and advice immediately. When you go home you can leave the worries behind. Home time is your own time and unless you are particularly talented at dealing with stress you will need it. Keeping home sacred is an important decision. Being a shoulder to cry on is a very rewarding job but it is a very exhausting one too. Everyone needs a place in their lives where they can be themselves. Patients often have unrealistic expectations of their practitioner and living up to these 24 hours a day can be hard. Also, it is rare in the life of a patient that contact with a practitioner is a life or death matter that cannot wait until the following day.

The Disadvantages

The drawbacks of renting space in a clinic as opposed to working from home are both personal and business oriented. A serious worry is the owner of the lease or the landlord's ability to put up the rent when he feels like it. You may have budgeted your practice very carefully only to find you have a rent increase at the end of the quarter or year which takes you completely by surprise. There is nothing you can do about this but to look elsewhere for room space or revise your fees.

Life's vagaries like political changes (remember the enormous rise in business rates after the introduction of the Community Charge?) always hit the vulnerable harder and as a practitioner renting space you are most vulnerable. You may have no say at all over the lease or the terms of it when it is renewed.

What you can do is check the terms on which you rent your space. Is the building a freehold or leasehold? If it is a leasehold, how long does the lease run for? When are the rent reviews? If they are fairly frequent then what is the owner's past record on increases and when do they occur? How do rent increases affect individuals like yourself who are only renting space and who do not own the lease? And so on. Do not be embarrassed by these sticky financial questions. You are a professional with a responsibility to yourself to know these things. You cannot be a good practitioner if you are constantly worried about money.

When you do rent space, find out if you are entering into any contractual arrangements or obligations. Do you have to help with the redecorating? If you sell any of the clinic's herbs, homeopathic remedies, vitamin pills, tonics etc. will you be given any commission or percentage? If not, you should find your own suppliers. This is not to be mercenary but to be business-like again. After all, you have to pay rent for time spent in the clinic. Therefore, you have to generate an income from that time. Time consequently does become linked to money and must be spent wisely.

Find out if the rent covers furnishings or are you going to be asked to contribute extra money for a new carpet or desk? If you enter a joint partnership in unfurnished premises and all the partners contribute towards the fixtures, fittings and furniture, what happens when a partner leaves? Does he lose his investment or is he compensated by the in-coming practitioner? If so, how do you work out depreciation?

Be absolutely sure of these aspects when you enter an agreement. If you sign anything be totally familiar with all the details of what you sign. Read carefully and digest. Do not assume that agreements are written in stone. There is always room for negotiation. Talk things through. The worst misunderstandings occur when people do not talk to each other. These can so often be avoided by simply sitting down and diplomatically facing any problem areas or disagreements. These are invaluable skills in the business world. We also recommend that you get advice from a reputable solicitor before signing any agreement and especially in regard to any serious business disputes. A solicitor's time is never cheap but you may find in the end that it saves you money and pain. Knowing your legal position is important in business and a powerful weapon when your livelihood is being threatened.

Another difficulty of renting space in a clinic which is already established is that you will have to fit into the image of the clinic. You may not like the way the clinic is decorated or the room layout. It may be too formal and cold for your style of practice. It may be too relaxed and untidy on the other hand. In other words, you have no say and that may irk you in time.

Worse still, you may find a curious mixture of personalities in the clinic that appear workable initially but, in the fullness of time, prove otherwise. We have known some practices where cold wars have raged for long periods of time. You may disagree with the way a practitioner works in a professional sense. He may cling on to patients long after they are cured to keep the fees rolling in, or he may reach dead ends in therapy and not refer that patient to others. You may find there are disagreements over money. It may be silly things like a therapist being untidy or forgetting to invoice remedies properly. It may relate to over-ordering of stock. Whatever the cause, the effects are disagreeable and unpleasant. One would hope that practitioners in natural medicine would be more enlightened about conflict, but they are human. Be sure that you are going to fit into the clinic you choose to work in and be wary of being drawn into conflicts which do not concern or affect you.

An example of this is when a therapist confuses bookings from home and in the clinic. The therapist has already filled the time with an appointment arranged from home. The receptionist has not been informed of the new patient and unknowingly double-books another patient in the allotted time. The receptionist then has to face an irate patient because of the therapist's thoughtless inefficiency. You may find yourself in the middle of a bad atmosphere which is nothing to do with you.

Other Considerations

Another problem that we hope you *will* encounter is one of becoming too busy and running out of appointment time. You may take one day a week and find you need two. If you are lucky, time to expand into will be there. If you are not you may find you have a busy schedule and not enough room to see everyone. The clinic, too, is busy and cannot spare you more time. You can do housecalls to ease the pressure and bide your time. Situations change and practitioners move on. A space may open for you. Otherwise you might have to move on yourself. Being successful has to be the best reason for change.

A Note For Fledgling Practitioners

Because of varying personal circumstances, it may not be possible for the fledgling practitioner to practise from a clinic immediately he qualifies, nor to work from home. Or if he finds he only has limited time in premises with more patients to see than this time allows, his enthusiasm may begin to wane.

One way around this problem is to start an itinerant practice, travelling to the homes of patients on one or two days a week, the weekends or evenings perhaps, to allow the business to continue building up. Obviously this must be arranged efficiently and take into account the geographical area covered and travelling costs. Patients can be grouped together in appointments according to where they live. It is important to do this with housecalls otherwise you may quickly find yourself losing money and not making it. Arranged efficiently, this system is a good way to establish a financial foundation which will help the change over period to a full week's work in clinics. It also creates a pool of patients to bring to the new venue, rather than paying for accommodation and waiting for appointments to fill the day. Most important, it encourages rather than frustrates the wave of confidence with which we leave the safety and comfort of *alma mater* to make our way in the world.

Chapter 4

BUYING A CLINIC WITH A PATIENT LIST

THE ADVANTAGES:
Instant patients. Excellent way to expand existing business or start from scratch if you have the capital. Inheriting goodwill and reputation by association. Credibility: therapist who is selling is entrusting you with his patient list. Change over time with advice from established therapist.

THE DISADVANTAGES:
Requires confidence to take on full time practice. Inevitable loss of some patients loyal to departing practitioner. Initial outlay is expensive. Practice may be shaped in a way you do not want to work. Prescribing or therapy techniques may differ. Compromises may be required to suit existing patients. Inheriting a bad reputation. A difference in philosophy or religion between previous and successive practitioners.

OTHER CONSIDERATIONS:
Getting to know the practitioner you are taking over from. Sitting in on consultations before taking over. Valuing the practice and example. Letter of introduction and example. Inheriting stock, remedies, accounts systems, furniture etc. Few hidden expenses.

The Advantages

The main advantage of buying a clinic with a patient list is that you can begin practising straight away. You have a place to work from with instant patients. This option is very desirable to the experienced practitioner who wishes to expand his catchment area. However if you are newly qualified, have the confidence and financial backing to afford this option, then go ahead and explore the situation. Opportunities do crop up from time to time and should be taken, whenever possible.

Inevitably practitioners may choose to move area or are coming up to retirement age and need someone to take on their practice. That someone could be you. In our own case, we had the good fortune to hear through the grapevine that a well-known local therapist was about to retire and was looking for someone to take over his clinic. We made the initial telephone call and arranged a meeting. As he practised from home, the deal was to include buying his bungalow as well as the patient list. He wanted to be nearer his family in Dorset and at that time we were already thinking of moving house, so we agreed to proceed with matters at our leisure. With two other clinics plus this one, we now had a very full working week.

Besides acquiring tangible assets by buying a patient list and practice, there are many intangible advantages which come with the arrangement. Obviously, you have instant patients and do not have to scout around for clients. You also inherit the 'goodwill' of your predecessor. If he has entrusted the practice which has been built up over years to you, then you, by implication, must be competent and trustworthy. The practitioner is hardly going to sell up to someone he does not consider competent unless he is completely unscrupulous. You inherit a reputation by association.

With goodwill comes credibility. Your new patients will naturally trust someone who has been handed the keys of the kingdom! This is invaluable to any practitioner, however seasoned. There is no price on these positive affirmations. No amount of money can buy goodwill, trust, credibility and competence and they are quickly lost by an uncaring incompetent.

There is also a bonus to the handing over period. Some colleges offer clinical experience or 'sitting in' with experienced therapists to their students but after graduation the opportunity does not come again. If your business arrangement includes a time when you are able to sit in with the retiring practitioner and watch him at work, all the better. We have both benefited over the years from watching experienced therapists at work. There is always a phenomenal amount to be learnt in these situations which is of great worth, however experienced you may be yourself. Everyone has individual skills and the experience of years can be nothing short of illuminating. It can be marvellously inspiring to watch a healer at work. This is a way to start a practice on a 'high'.

The Disadvantages

On the minus side, there are aspects to be considered. It does require confidence to take on a clinic. You will encounter disappointment from patients who were comfortable with your predecessor and do not like change. You will inevitably lose patients who do not want to see you. Expect to lose at least a third of the patients but do not worry, these will be replenished in the first year. This loss of clients will be kept to a minimum by a handing over letter, discussed in detail a few pages further on.

You must accept that patient loyalty may be short lived because of your different approach to practising and they may not be comfortable with your techniques. The practice may have operated in a way that you are unable to sustain. Your prescribing habits may be radically different. Do you adapt your techniques to accommodate the patients or require that they change for you? These decisions can only be yours. Full knowledge of what you are taking on and careful thought are essential.

Buying a patient list with a house is also expensive, especially in a financial climate with high interest rates and high inflation. If you already own property which is saleable, this may not present a problem. Do your sums well and do not be over optimistic when deciding on the transaction. 'Decide in haste and repent at leisure.' Incidentally, if premises you purchase are also where you live then the chapter on *Working From Home*, will be worth rereading.

There is also the matter of bad reputations. It would be very sad to acquire an apparent bargain practice only to discover that your predecessor had a very bad reputation in the community. It is *always* wise to investigate thoroughly all aspects of what you are taking on. A chat at the local health food shop or with other therapists in the area could save you much pain and money.

Finally, personal beliefs can be a stumbling block. If your predecessor is a 'Born Again Christian' and places a great emphasis on his spiritual beliefs at work this could pose a problem to the Buddhist successor! The patients may expressly prefer a religious slant in the practice. Again, find out how the land lies and think the whole acquisition through very carefully.

Other Considerations

A point worth considering is that you need to spend some time to get to know the practitioner you are taking over from to establish trust and confidence on both sides. He needs to be happy with you before entrusting you with his patients. You need to be sure that you will feel comfortable taking over his patient list and working with people who have a loyalty to your predecessor. You won't be able to introduce the new broom without causing a great deal of resentment and there will be aspects of the old practice that will have to be initially accepted. You will not be able to change everything at once without losing precisely the list you have invested in.

Initially you need to visit frequently to go through case notes, to discuss and even more important to 'sit in' on some of the consultations to get the feel of how the practitioner/therapist works. Their style or technique may be completely different from yours, so it is important to know at first hand what you are dealing with. To help the patient with the transition from one practitioner to another, it would be useful if your style/technique was not too dissimilar from your predecessor, initially anyway, to make the patient as comfortable as possible with the new situation. If the difference of style/technique is too great you may need to reconsider. One of the many fears that may present itself at this time is: 'What if they don't stay?' 'What if they don't like me?' If you have satisfied yourself with the financial set up, the style/technique situation, you should work through such fears and proceed.

In our case, the transition from one practitioner to another went very well, and the price that we paid for the patient list has paid for itself many times over. In our opinion, if you have the means, then consider this option as a good choice to make.

The price of a patient list can vary from one to seven times the annual turn over. In our case we bought a freehold with residential living space but you could equally well find a clinic on a leasehold with a patient list. The normal basis for a valuation of a practice would be to take a straight average of three years' fees and apply a capital factor, normally of approximately 1.25, to arrive at a valuation. If, however, the practice has grown enormously in the three years considered, then the weighted average of the turn over for those three years up to the last year would be taken and a capital factor applied to that. The weighted mean average is calculated by multiplying the first year's turn over by one, the second year by two and the third by three. The total is divided by six (the sum of the three year's weighted mean averages) to give the weighted average value. This in turn is then multiplied by the capital value of the practice. For example:

WEIGHTED MEAN AVERAGE OF TURN OVER TO 31st AUGUST 1990

1988 Fees	£9,000.00	x 1	£9,000.00
1989 Fees	£10,500.00	x 2	£21,000.00
1990 Fees	£18,000.00	x 3	£54,000.00
			£84,000.00

Weighted Average Value:	£14,000.00
	£14,000.00 x 1.25
Capital Value of Practice =	£17,500.00

The sum of £17,500 would be considered the goodwill element attached to the practice. The freehold would, of course, be a separate matter. These figures are not applicable to every clinic and do not take into account a business with high overheads but they are a useful example. Professional advice is again essential before investing in any business.

Before taking over the practice, make sure that you get a letter of introduction from your predecessor. If it is typed get him to handsign his signature on all the copies. It will be in your interest to address, stamp and send the letters in the post as soon as possible to inform patients of their practitioner's departure and your arrival on the scene. There is nothing worse than patients phoning up to make an appointment only to find their normal practitioner has moved away without saying goodbye. Then they are confronted with a strange practitioner whom they have never met. You! If you follow this procedure you will avoid such a scenario. Patients/clinics are touchingly loyal to their therapists who often become like a surrogate member of the family over the years. To abandon them without warning will not give the new person filling the practice shoes a sporting chance.

We offer you an example of the sort of letter required:

> *Dear Patient*
>
> *I am writing to inform you that I am retiring from my practice at the Excellent Natural Health Centre and I am moving to the West Country.*
>
> *I have handed over my practice to Mr A who is available for consultation all day on Tuesdays and Fridays.*
>
> *Mr A will be happy to continue to see you and looks forward to meeting you. He is currently practising in the nearby towns of Y and Z in a style similar to my own. He was an obvious choice to succeed me. In addition to his Chiropractic skills, he is a qualified Nutritionist and also specialises in the treatment of sports injuries.*
>
> *My successor, Mr A, will of course retain all the relevant files, notes and X-rays relating to the practice to ensure that the change over period will not inconvenience any patient.*
>
> *I would like to thank you for your support over the years and wish you all the very best for the future.*
>
> *Yours sincerely,*

Incidentally, we have found that dentists do not seem to have a particularly good reputation for informing their patients of changes in the practice. Most people are apprehensive about going to the dentist, and once they feel comfortable with one (who does not hurt!) they like to stay with him forever. If he 'ups sticks' and goes without even letting you know or informing you about his brilliant successor, the latter does not stand a chance in keeping the old patients. Do not underestimate the loyalty patients hold to one practitioner and the distress caused by his departure.

When you buy the premises and patient list together, you may be able to purchase the clinic furniture and fittings. This will obviously be a big plus factor for the patients, as this will all help to create the image of continuity for them. It is also a plus factor for you as office furniture is horrendously expensive, even when acquired second hand. You may acquire book cases, shelving, couches, chairs, a telephone system, filing cabinets, desks, medicine cabinets, etc. All these items could be of great use to you and available at reasonable prices. They may even be part of the practice acquisition.

Besides acquiring furniture, you will inherit an accounts system which may well be a great help if you are starting up straight out of college. If you are fortunate, it will be an efficient system which you are able to dovetail into with ease. You will possibly wish to modify it to your own ways in time but it is a secure start in the world of figures.

To many, accounts are a nightmare and we know of many instances of businesses not keeping up with accounts on a regular basis and then encountering a mad panic at the end of the financial year. Creating accounts which are old history is a nightmare as one invariably loses unfiled essential receipts in the process of time. We cannot stress too strongly: find a reasonably priced accountant with a good reputation before you start your business. Do not wait until the end of the year and keep your records on a regular basis. Then accounts are a chore and not a nightmare. But more of the detail of accounting systems later on.

In terms of 'hardware', furniture and accounts are not the only possible acquisitions. You may be lucky enough to inherit a thriving business which supplies herbs, Bach Flower Remedies, homeopathic tinctures and remedies, vitamins, minerals, aromatherapy oils, relaxation tapes, books, Chinese medicinal herbs, elixirs and other delights of the apothecary. The outgoing practitioner may leave this stock as part of the acquisition price or you may have to buy them as an extra. Whatever the arrangement, this mail order and patient supply business is another way of generating revenue which could be a wonderful bonus to the fledgeling therapist.

Although it is tempting to redecorate and change the practice room, we advise that you leave it exactly as it is for the first six months to allow the patients to get to know the strange 'you' in familiar surroundings.

In addition to fittings and stock, the outgoing practitioner may wish to offer you such medicinal equipment as opthalmoscopes, stethoscopes, sphygmomanometers, ear syringes, surgical bowls, biofeedback machines, iridology camera and tripod, or a diagnostic computer with materia medica. Obviously, each individual practice will offer different opportunities. Make sure you negotiate fair prices for each item and do not be persuaded to pay over the odds for anything because you are being offered a good patient list.

Whatever the individual circumstances, you will find that an arrangement of this nature does not have hidden costs which you have not anticipated. You pay for the practice and possibly the property. Everything else should be negotiable

THE RAWORTH CENTRE

COLLEGE FOR SPORTS THERAPY AND NATURAL MEDICINE

The Raworth College, established in 1983 has built up an enviable reputation for excellence in training standards. It offers a comprehensive range of training in two major areas – Sports Therapy and Natural Medicine, although Combined Studies courses can be arranged.

Education is available on a full-time or part-time basis, and courses range from those designed for a complete beginner to opportunities for practising professionals to extend their expertise into new modalities. Vacation courses and some week-end study programmes are also offered.

DEPARTMENT OF NATURAL THERAPY

• NATURAL HEALTH PRACTITIONERS DIPLOMA – 1 Year full-time.
A number of related therapies, securely based on Anatomy and Physiology, Pathology and Oriental approaches.

• DIPLOMA IN HOLISTIC AROMATHERAPY– 3 months full-time,
or 6 months part time.
A full career preparation course, and one for which the Raworth College is justly famous.

• DIPLOMA COURSES IN Acupressure, Reflexology, Nutritional Therapy, Applied Kinesiology, and Therapeutic Massage.

DEPARTMENT OF SPORTS THERAPY

• MASTERS DIPLOMA IN SPORTS THERAPY– 1 Year full-time.
Combined studies in Sports Injury rehabilitation, Fitness Testing and Corrective treatments, Sports Psychology, Massage and Sports Conditioning.

• INTERNATIONAL DIPLOMA IN HEALTH AND SPORTS THERAPY –
6 months full-time.
Fitness teaching and Gym Work, Injury management, Anatomy and Physiology, Nutrition, Sauna and sunbed operation.

• DIPLOMA COURSES IN Health and Fitness Studies, Gym Instruction, Aerobic Fitness Teaching, Sports Massage.

Prospectus with details of all courses offered by the Centre available from:
The Raworth Centre, "Smallburgh", Beare Green,
Dorking, Surrey, RH5 4QA.
TEL: 0306 - 712623

as we have mentioned. This way, it is easy to work out what you can afford and hopefully not run into difficulties further down the road.

Despite the pitfalls, buying a patient list and practice can be a marvellous boost to a practitioner who wishes to start up from scratch or expand. We can confidently reiterate that, in our case, the transition from one practitioner to another went very well, and the price we paid for the patient list has paid for itself many times over. Furthermore, it has been a pleasurable challenge moulding our approach onto an established practice without alienating valued patients.

Chapter 5

LEASING PREMISES

THE ADVANTAGES:
Ability to bring in other practitioners. Cost sharing. Colleagues standing in as receptionists for each other in the early days. Joint publicity lectures. Exhibitions and courses.
THE DISADVANTAGES:
Expensive option. Paying rent. Vulnerable to landlord's whims. Reliance on other practitioners.
OTHER CONSIDERATIONS:
Being the boss. Housecalls. Competition from other practitioners. A note on appearance.

The Advantages

Leasing premises is the initial way to start up in business for a large number of practitioners. If the premises are large enough, you may be able to invite other practitioners to work with you. This is always a pleasing situation to be in, for several reasons. It is good to work amongst colleagues for friendship, company and support. You will be able to share expenses in setting up the business to include furniture and fittings, carpets, curtains, decorations, a telephone system and any specialist equipment that may be necessary. As we have already said, an answer phone is essential. Although most people have some reservations about using them, it has to be a facility available for use when no one is around to answer calls from patients. Answer phones can pay for themselves in a very short period of time, taking useful messages which may be lost otherwise. They will also contribute to the clinic's efficient and professional image.

Inviting other practitioners to share your clinic not only helps with the obvious overheads, but it also has the advantage that someone can be available at the clinic to book appointments when you are not there or when you are in consultation (and vice versa). Receptionists are essential, but in your first year so is bread and butter, so you will probably have to double up as practitioner/receptionist for a while until you can afford one. Sharing reception with another practitioner is a solution. One can do the accounts and catch up on administrative jobs whilst the other is seeing clients. For hypnotherapists this system or an answer phone is essential. You can't book patients and develop trance states at the same time! Generally, it is more relaxing not to be distracted whilst in full flow and clients deserve your undivided attention. After all, they are paying for it!

Another advantage of working with other practitioners is that you are able to share publicity ventures with them. You may wish to hire a stand at an exhibition or share a series of lectures or courses at the local adult education centre. Colleagues can also help you design and distribute leaflets and cards in the area and share the cost of advertising. Local papers are also more predisposed to writing about a natural health centre rather than one individual working alone. However, new practitioners do need to be aware of advertising restrictions. Many colleges prefer that their graduates do not advertise or at least restrict the wording of their advertisements to what is on their business cards. New practitioners do need referrals to survive and students should be aware of this from the onset of their training. They may spend four years paying fees and three years establishing a practice. That is a long haul to prosperity!

The Disadvantages

Acquiring short lease premises is an expensive option and does not have the advantage of any form of investment. All your rent is paid out regularly but you do not even have a lease to sell on when you decide to leave. The whims of landlords can be fickle so it is always advisable to let your solicitor peruse the lease agreement to his satisfaction. Beware of hidden extras like unreasonable maintenance agreements and too many dates for possible rent reviews. Read the small print. You want to know that you cannot be ousted from the property without good reason and a period of notice. Be aware also that your lease requires a commitment in terms of time, e.g. 3, 5 or 10 years. If you want to get out of the lease agreement, you may find it difficult to sell on to another practitioner and you may lose a lot of money by pulling out because the landlord then has to spend time and money finding another tenant.

Public liability insurance for the premises (indeed for any clinic you set up) will also be necessary which will protect your patients or other visitors should they meet with any accidents whilst on your premises. We deal with all aspects of insurance in Chapter 16.

Change of use to medical consulting rooms will need to be applied for from the relevant planning authorities. The procedure is as follows: draw up plans of the interior of the property, submit them to the planning authorities and write a letter explaining your case. If the property is new and is previously unused you will still need a change of use unless it is built specifically for medical consulting rooms. If the property is residential you will need to do the same if you are sharing with other practitioners who do not live there. The estate agent who normally negotiates on behalf of the leasor will usually know someone in the local planning department and will be able to get a 'feel' for whether a change of use will be granted. Take advantage of his experience and contacts. Estate agents can sometimes obtain planning permission on properties that the average person would not stand a chance of achieving on his own. Some problems that you may encounter are outlined in the following chapter.

Other Considerations

You may want to take full responsibility for the setting up costs yourself and charge a rent to practitioners on a daily rate basis. This method seems the most popular in many clinics around the country. It affords you complete control over decisions of running policy, decoration of the premises and who you allow to practise in the clinic. It also means you hold the financial reins, for good or bad, and you will have to weather any storms which may arise. If you feel confident in the clinic's success, this will not be a problem but make sure you have a comprehensive business plan with accurate cashflow forecasts before you shoulder the responsibility all on your own. Many good businesses fail in the first year before they have the opportunity to establish themselves because they lack cash to ride out the lean times. The lean times are often August and December although this does vary from clinic to clinic and between the disciplines.

It is also dependent on your personality. You may need to control your business exclusively or you may need the support, financial and otherwise, of other colleagues. There is nothing wrong with either option, as long as you are clear about your needs and structure the business accordingly. Relationships fray when people try to be what they are not. If you want to be the boss and crack the whip do so. As long as your clinic is efficient, fair and offers a good service to practitioners and patients alike there is nothing wrong with this method. On the other hand, it is valuable to have good partners. They can strengthen the business and help run it. The emphasis is on *good*, however. Sharing the responsibility allows you to go on holiday with a clearer mind. (Leaving a business is always a concern.) There are drawbacks, of course, and we deal with these and the subject of contracts of agreement fully in the next chapter.

In our own particular case, our very first clinic was set up in this way. For a good many years we paid a considerable amount of rent to a very happy landlord. (We remember it well!) We took out a lease on two rooms on the first floor in a historical city in the south of England. The rooms were adequate in size and, with our newly acquired £5000 bank loan, we set about carpeting, furnishing and decorating the consulting and waiting rooms respectively.

Being on the first floor was not ideal, but as property for rent was in such demand, we decided to tempt fate and carry on anyway. The rooms did have the advantage of being in a convenient central position in the city and were light and airy. If we had waited for the perfect time and perfect premises to materialise, we would have never made the all important first step. Looking back, most patients were able to negotiate the stairs with not too much difficulty and we offered housecalls to those who clearly could not. But whenever possible rent a property on the ground floor or with a lift (although be prepared to pay more for this). Many disabled clients do not want to be treated differently and welcome the opportunity to go out into the world. Housecalls are also time consuming and require extra transport costs. Do you pay the petrol and time or does your client because your clinic is inaccessible?

When inviting other practitioners to work under the same roof, do not be put off if they practise the same discipline as yourself. Competition is always healthy, and both parties usually end up by gaining. Do not be put off if you also find that a similar practitioner/therapist has an established clinic around the corner from you. This was the case with our first clinic.

A doctor with an established practice had been working in the same therapy just around the corner from us for many years. He managed to fit in two days a fortnight in between his Channel Islands and London clinics. This was a

threatening situation for anyone without a £5000 bank loan, never mind someone with one. As it happened, this seemingly intolerable situation turned to our favour. Because the doctor was so often not to be found in the local clinic but in his exotic Channel Islands location, some of his patients wanted someone who was more accessible. This was true of those patients with young children who tend to suffer from more acute complaints that can blow up in hours. We were the obvious choice, especially as we were just around the corner. The good doctor had promoted our shared therapy in the city and then left enough room for us to take advantage of his absence.

We were also very different in our therapeutic approach. The doctor saw a great number of patients in a day with a short period of time allotted for each case. We preferred to spend more time with each individual and had a greater role as counsellor as well as working within our specialised form of natural medicine. Of course, some of the doctor's clients required that their practitioner was a medical doctor. As we are professional therapists we could never fill these shoes but we worked happily side by side and both practised with great success. What could have been a totally threatening situation for us was in fact completely harmonious and continued for many years.

Being in a prime city centre location is always a plus factor as it is easy for patients to find you, usually with the added bonus of public transport to get them to you without too much trouble. But do not expect to find a property of this kind on the cheap. They never are. Landlords are well aware of the value of convenience and good communication lines. You pay for these privileges.

A Note on Appearance

We are aware that we mention *image* fairly frequently. In an ideal world, appearance would be relatively unimportant. Veneer is nothing to do with the wood below. However, in our image conscious age patients do look at details to assess the competence of the practitioner. Appearing to be professional, though it is obviously not as fundamental as *being* professional, is important to win over the trust and confidence of clients from the onset. If this is partly done by the practitioner's tidy professional appearance and surroundings, all the better. There is no point in working against yourself when you can work for yourself. We know of practitioners who do lose patients because they are dressed untidily or because their surroundings are not up to scratch. No one in business can afford to lose custom for this reason which requires very little effort to remedy. It also helps the self confidence to be well dressed oneself and to work in a pleasant environment.

Chapter 6

BUYING A LONG LEASE

Multi-therapy clinics. 'Change of use' and the planning authorities. Parking facilities. Mortgages. Limited companies. Partnership agreements. Solicitors. Case history. Design, decoration and layout. Tiny terrors and teethmarks.

Many of the advantages and disadvantages of buying a long lease are similar to those already discussed in the previous two chapters. In this chapter we therefore review the considerations particular to acquiring a long lease. The main difference to buying a long lease is that it locks you into a system of ownership for a specified lengthy period of time. This has the advantage of giving you an investment which you can sell on providing, of course, that you can find a buyer. This is always dependent on market forces. Buying a long lease is an excellent way of starting a clinic, particularly a multi-therapy practice. However, it is a big responsibility and one that must be considered carefully before any commitment.

The main difficulties, perhaps, are that this approach requires substantial capital (as with buying a freehold) and, more to the point, a 'change of use' for the premises is required, unless it has specifically been built as medical consulting rooms. This has to be granted by the relevant planning authorities which can be a problem.

The main obstacle to granting the change of use is usually parking facilities. If you can acquire a property with plenty of room for practitioners' and visiting patients' cars, you may be in with a chance. The planning authorities always seem to be concerned with the nuisance value of a new scheme and what the reaction of the neighbours will be. In a commercial centre this obviously plays a smaller role in the decision and planning permission will go through quickly, all being well.

In a residential area converting an entire building is far more difficult. It is easier to maintain a proportion of residential space in the building and convert the rest to business use. Unfortunately, it is unlikely that a purely residential leasehold would have a long enough lease or have provision to allow such a change. You are more likely to change the use of a residential freehold. This is an even more expensive option than a leasehold and necessitates a large investment. Before the property market slumped we could have happily written that despite the outlay, as long as you had the means to repay the mortgage, you were on to a winner. You simply could not lose. We know of instances in which commercial property *tripled* in value in a matter of four years. The mortgage repayments became minimal in comparison to the market value of the bricks and mortar. Much of this value was related to the position of the property, the surrounding businesses of course, and not the actual state of repair.

Today, the picture is very different. It would be a good gamble to acquire a mortgage with a fixed interest rate, the rates being what they are in the 1990s. Even with the political carrot of general elections, we cannot rely on interest rates going down in our present economic climate. The Western world is less stable than it wishes to appear. Mortgages without a fixed rate are also speculative and unless the investor has a large slice of capital, the repayments could be crippling to the practice. A clinic has to see an awful lot of clients to generate enough income to repay a £60,000 mortgage comfortably, even if it is available. Freehold commercial property is expensive, despite the depressed state of the market. £60,000 would not buy much, although property prices vary enormously despite the slump and depending on where you are located.

For these reasons, a long lease may be a possible option as it is cheaper than a freehold property. The lease, though a greater responsibility, is an investment (given that prices do not slump further!) which you may wish to sell on when you have established a successful multi-therapy natural health clinic. You may also find that property developers, banks and estate agents are more willing to offer you good deals precisely because the market is depressed and they need your business far more than you need them. Shop around and push for good prices on everything. They can afford to compromise. You cannot.

To Limit or Not To Limit?

Another option is to run your practice as a limited company registered in the UK with shareholders and directors. This effectively limits the liability of the business to a degree should you go bankrupt and run up huge debts. That is the advantage. The disadvantages are many. Limited companies cost up to £300 to set up (unless you buy one on the cheap 'off the shelf'. If you take this option make sure there are no clauses in the Memorandum and Articles which may limit your ability to trade in certain areas and ways). Limited companies also require that the directors pay a larger contribution of national insurance than self-employed partners by operating under the Pay As You Earn system and the tax concessions are not as good. Your company status may cost you thousands of pounds a year in insurance contributions and tax. If your individual insurance policies protect you from being sued by patients you may have no reason at all to invest in a limited company. However, a good accountant can brief you fully on this subject.

Partnership Agreements and Solicitors

You may consider going into a partnership with other practitioners to help finance and run the clinic. This could be set up as a business partnership or as a cooperative. For a partnership you will need a partnership agreement which a solicitor must draw up, stating the amount of money each partner has invested in the venture and the breakdown of percentage of ownership each has acquired. This makes the whole venture business-like, fair and legal. We cannot stress too strongly the importance of having everything in black and white. So many relationships have gone profoundly sour in business. Without being pessimistic, we know of more disagreements between business partners than marital breakdowns. Partnerships are, in many ways, more difficult to manage than marriages because the offspring is mostly monetary, not flesh, and there is very little romance to ease the way! But to start off on a realistic and sensible footing will always stack the odds in your favour.

You may feel that paying solicitors to draw up such an agreement is an unwanted expense. Professional fees do vary and it is worth shopping around. Partnership agreements should be standard to most solicitors unless they are purely involved in property conveyancing. Check out your solicitor's going rate and services. He should give you an indication of how much the agreement and the acquisition of the lease should cost. Do not be afraid to question the document if it does not suit your need or if it has taken an unreasonable amount of time or money to draw up. However, it is always a good insurance to use a solicitor and spend a few hundred pounds for his professional advice rather than to do things on the cheap yourself and to lament the loss of thousands of pounds later on due to some detail you have missed. Incidently, solicitors are not fool-proof and they have been known to make mistakes. Legal jargon can make them seem or sound intimidating. One of the biggest problems with legal documents is the lack of punctuation. Take a deep breath and wade through every word. Remember that you are the customer and that the solicitor is employed by you.

Also, as with any document you choose to sign in your life, read it and make sure you understand all the clauses down to the last detail. Who is contracted to do the maintenance on the property? Are all the partners' names on the lease and therefore subject to any agreements drawn up? Are there any hidden or ambiguous clauses which may trip you up after you have signed with the current owners of the lease/partners in the business? Are you absolutely clear about the conditions of all arrangements? This should include whether there is a peppercorn rent (a nominal sum paid each year for the lease). Is it subject to review? How long is the lease? Can it be withdrawn under any circumstances? And so on. The world is sadly full of sharks waiting for tender, kind and innocent people to walk into their cavernous jaws to be eaten. We speak from bitter experience. Do not be taken in by charming, charismatic salesmen, offering apparently unmissable deals! Remember, there is no such thing as a 'free lunch'. Find a reputable solicitor and stick with him. He may save you much heartache and financial pain but make sure he is not too much of a charming, charismatic salesman himself!

To see an example of a partnership agreement, please refer to the Appendix at the end of the book.

Make sure that your partnership agreement allows you to release yourself from such a contract should any unforeseen circumstances arise. For example, a practitioner went into partnership with two others to buy the lease of a new property to be converted to a natural health centre. They decided that should any partner wish to leave the clinic within three years they would have to accept only the money they had invested up until that point and not the market value of the property. The remaining partners then had the option of purchasing their share. They agreed on this proposal because they realised that it would take extremely hard work to get the clinic established in the early years. Any disruption at that delicate time would have to carry some sort of penalty as it would have placed undue financial pressure on the partners remaining loyal to the project. (This occurred in the mid 1980s when property prices were escalating at a phenomenal rate due to easy credit and massive inflation in the marketplace.) It gave the project a sporting chance to survive, despite the possible shadow of disagreement.

Within the first two years, one of the partners did decide to leave the practice. The remaining two only had to pay back his investment to date and not the actual market value of the property which had increased considerably in a short period of time. Obviously, in a deflationary market this arrangement would present more of a risk to the remaining partners but it is a risk that is preferable to paying the market value for a clinic which is well beyond your means. The partner who wishes to leave could always look for an investor from outside the partnership if you are unwilling to pay. The disadvantage of this is that you cannot choose this person. You may end up with an unhappy 'arranged marriage'. Of course, you should have a contract which protects you from a partner selling to an unknown or unsuitable person.

Our own experience in this field was happy. A number of therapists got together with a reasonable sum of capital to invest between them. We were

seeking a property in which to start a clinic encompassing many natural therapies. We had had a number of applications for change of use to various residential properties turned down by the planning authorities. This was attributed to the bugbear of parking space. We eventually came across a newly built two storey building with individual units for sale on a long lease. The unit was finally partitioned into three consulting rooms with all the necessary fixtures such as telephone extensions and hand wash basins with a reception area for waiting clients. The building was close to the railway station and the bus station. Most important, it was in the centre of the city and easily accessible for disabled as well as able-bodied clients and, to mollify the planning authorities, there was a large car park in the courtyard outside! This meant that patients could drive there or be dropped off right outside the door. Communication lines were good. We were not stuck out in the sticks miles from anywhere and remote from public transport. These factors of layout for the disabled and accessibility for all are essential factors in the success of any clinic.

The set up of our clinic was ideal. In fact, it was a personal goal of all of us to own a clinic which housed different therapies, all working under the same roof. We were providing a much needed health centre in the centre of a prosperous city which offered a wide range of different therapies. It was also a good investment for us with no greedy landlord breathing down our necks with crippling rent increases and maintenance levies.

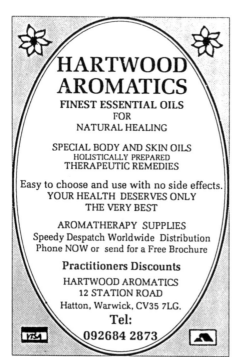

Entering into such a business partnership does take courage and it is a challenge. There is a great deal of responsibility involved, working together and meeting mortgage repayments. However, it does allow you a tremendous amount of freedom to run the business in your own way without the restrictions of a short lease landlord. You can decorate the place with whatever colours you wish, hang curtains or blinds of your design and create the image and atmosphere you desire.

We consider it essential to make the patient feel relaxed and calm whilst in the clinic and certain colours, designs and decorations can enhance feelings of calm and security in subtle, understated ways. Research has categorically proved that red rooms increase blood pressure, pink rooms create a sense of well-being and calm; room layouts either welcome or inhibit visitors and patterns and shapes elicit standard responses from a wide variety of people. The psychology behind all this is well documented but we would agree that much of this knowledge is intuitive. Experiment in your clinics and ask each other for individual opinions. Setting up your practice rooms should be well thought out but enjoyable, a chance for you to express individuality as a therapist.

For many people, the idea of going into a clinic is not an alien one as most doctor's surgeries are run in this way. One can have a natural health centre without it being soulless and clinical. It can be welcoming and personalised without losing a sense of efficiency or professionalism.

Tiny Terrors and Teeth-marks

One of the dangers of being too attached to your beautiful, newly decorated clinic is the inevitability of the public coming in and wrecking it, particularly the smaller members of the public. It is not always sweetness and light when treating young children and it is necessary to see and hear the child rather than rely on the parents' observations. A colleague of ours seemed to attract particularly troublesome, active and aggressive children and his immaculate consulting rooms were frequently upturned. After one particular visitor, he discovered a set of teeth marks in his desk! On another occasion a little two year old boy, who had been accompanying his mother to a consultation with another therapist in the adjoining consulting room, took it upon himself to explore the clinic. On seeing our colleague's soft high backed chair vacant, the boy promptly sat himself down and peed on it!

The moral of this tale is to always have a box of toys handy, plenty of tissues and a willing receptionist who can take over from mum or dad whilst they visit their therapist. Your patients who bring young children can warn you when they are coming so that the receptionist is prepared to lend a hand whilst the parents are in consultation. The system works well. Also keep expensive books and objects out of reach or else you will spend the whole of the consultation up and down like a jack-in-the-box, as not all parents can or are prepared to control their children. Expect drinks to be spilt, biscuits to be trodden into the carpet, sticky fingers grabbing at books, temper tantrums and the door being given a good kicking by an unwilling little patient or an unruly little accompaniment!

* * *

As with any venture, you need to be absolutely clear that you can work harmoniously with your partners and reach agreements, however heated the path to those agreements may be. Make sure all your agreements are well thought out and in writing. Do not rely on verbal agreements and goodwill. Outline the time and responsibility required for the clinic which is over and above your normal practice. Weigh this up very carefully if you already have family and personal responsibilities which take your time. Can you spare an extra evening a week for practitioner meetings, weekends cleaning and decorating the clinic and time spent on PR. All this could be the straw that breaks the camel's back. Ask yourself how many evenings do you have available at present. Are you committed to any administrative duties related to your own therapy and how much time does that take a month? How many evenings do you spend with your spouse and children and how many evenings do you have for yourself? Running a clinic, even with the cooperation of your business partners, will take an average of four to six hours a week.

As we have already mentioned, there can be many stumbling blocks in personal relationships in clinics. We know of instances where open war has broken out due to personality clashes, marital problems and differing attitudes to business. Hardly harmonious examples to set, but very human ones.

We are not suggesting that you write extra-marital affairs out of your contracts! What we are stressing is that people are fundamentally unreliable because life is full of unexpected happenings. Attempt to expect the unexpected and be wary of trusting any situation one hundred per cent. Put all your agreements, business plans and practices in writing. Be clear and have a financial/business strategy. 'Trust in God, but tie up your camel', as the old Arab saying goes.

Bear in mind that if you are working with other practitioners who are renting space from you, you will probably need to employ a receptionist if you are all too busy to provide that service yourself. Working with others can be profoundly fulfilling and creative if you have the right recipe of talent and personality. It can stretch and expand you in ways you could not contemplate on your own. Owning a clinic can be a tremendous investment which you may then sell on as a going concern with much financial reward in the future. It is also a security and an expression of your commitment to natural therapies. It is a service to the public and can be an excellent challenge in your professional life. If approached carefully, with planning and foresight, acquiring a long lease may be one of the best moves you could undertake.

Chapter 7

MONEY, MONEY, MONEY!

Borrowing money. Business plans and example. Profit forecasts and example. Cashflow charts and example. How to approach your bank manager. Obtaining a loan. Small business loans. Property finance and business mortgages. Free banking. Accounts and your accountant. Business accounts and example. Earning under £10,000 a year. What you can claim on the business. National Insurance contributions. VAT. What are you worth?

To acquire any of the options we have outlined, it will probably be necessary for you to borrow money at some stage. This should not present a stumbling block. If the proposition is a good one, then you should explore the pros and cons and the best way to finance such a venture.

Financial matters are an important part of being in business and need careful consideration. Your bank manager will be only too pleased to listen to your proposals. Before going to him make sure you are prepared and have as much information as you can collect. In short, have a business plan prepared. The more thorough and thought out, the better. The purpose of a business plan is to help you set down on paper everything that is involved in your venture. It will be a business blueprint of your ideas, not only to impress your bank manager, but as a point of reference to check on day to day decisions against your stated objectives. It is an essential document to draw upon whenever you discuss finances with bank managers, business partners, your accountant and anyone else interested in your welfare and plans for the future.

The business plan will include your skills, experience and qualifications. What type of business is it? What is the service? Do you intend to start a new business? Will it be sole trader, partnership or limited company (your accountant will advise)? Who do you see as your customers? What will you charge? Compare your prices with those of your competitors. What is the competition? Consider your premises; renting, leasing, working from home. When can you start? How much money do you have to survive on until the practice builds up? Can you join the Enterprise Allowance Scheme if you are registered as unemployed before starting up in practice? What are your running costs? Are there any hidden expenses like furniture or equipment? Do you have an emergency fund if your car goes on the blink? Do you have a marketing plan and the finance to carry it out? Do you need any equipment for your business? Do you intend to sell supplements, herbs or any other goods with your consultations? Have you considered whether you may be liable for VAT and do you know the law? (More on VAT later.)

Try to think of every angle, however small, that may relate to your practice and prepare thoroughly for this meeting. Do not be caught out by being unprepared.

You will need to take setting up costs into account, which are all 'one-offs' incurred when you first start up. Include everything you will need for acquiring and refurbishing premises, medical equipment, stock like vitamins or books and business essentials like stationery, account books, a cash box, a filing system. All these details add up to a considerable amount of money. People usually underestimate on start up costs and it is a wise move to add 20% to your figure to account for hidden expenses. Also your running costs will need to be listed. You have to pay these even if you produce, supply or sell nothing at all. These include rent, rates, light/heating, repairs/maintenance, telephone, insurance, vehicles, advertising and, of course, your salary.

For an example of a Business Plan, see pages 53-57.

After completing your business plan you will need to form a profit forecast or projected balance sheet. This will help you monitor your expected business performance month by month. How much can you afford to pay yourself? How much do you need? Its main purpose is, however, to show how viable your business is likely to be.

For an example of a Projected Balance Sheet/Profit Forecast, see pages 58-59.

Next on the list is your cashflow forecast. It will record the amount of cash expected in, and when you expect to pay it out again. It will form the basis of how much working capital you need month by month to keep the business going.

For an example of a Cashflow Statement/Forecast, see pages 60-64.

These details are essential. It is too easy to start up a business with a great deal of enthusiasm and very little concrete evidence of success and then go under within the first year. In 1989, there was a 10% increase in the failure of all new businesses started in that year as compared with the failure rate in the previous year, 1988. These are difficult economic times and success is only achieved by talent, business ability, excellent planning and 100% effort.

SMALL FIRMS
S E R V I C E

Business Plan, Projected Balance Sheet and Cashflow Statement on pages 53-64 have been reproduced with the kind permission of the Small Firms Service

BUSINESS PLAN

I. NATURE OF BUSINESS

a) Details of trading activities.

b) Date of commencement.

c) Expected date of commencement (new business only).

d) Formation (ie sole trader, partnership, limited company).

2. OWNERS/MANAGERS AND PRESENT COMMITMENTS

a) Short personal and business background including age, family commitment, qualifications, skills and experience.

b) Are you employed at present and what is your position? (New business only.)

3. OBJECTIVE

What do you/your business hope to achieve over the next few years?

4. MARKET

a) Describe the market you can serve.

b) Detail your product/service and offer any detail of the current competition.

4. MARKET (cont.)

c) Explain how you can achieve success in this market and better your competitors.

d) Describe how you plan to sell your product/service.

e) Who are/will be your major customers, and what indications have you got that they will buy from you?

f) What knowledge and experience have you of the industry you propose to enter?

5. PREMISES, PLANT, FITTINGS AND VEHICLES

a) **Premises**
Details of premises, freehold or leasehold, including internal floor space area, cost or annual rent or estimated cost or estimated rental and loan finance.

b) **Plant and fittings**
Details of present plant and fittings including estimated value and hire/lease purchase commitments.

Details of plant and fittings required including estimated cost.

c) **Vehicles**
Details of present vehicles including estimated value and hire purchase commitments.

Details of vehicles required including estimated cost.

6. FINANCE

a) Cash Flow Projection, Trading Forecast and Projected Balance sheet to be attached, and the principles on which they are based should be stated.

b) Existing business should also attach past three years' annual accounts.

c) Please add here any additional information which will help others understand your financial position.

7. INVESTMENT REQUIRED

Finance required for capital investment in premises, eg legal costs, surveys, alterations, architects' fees etc. .... £ _____

Finance required for working capital .... £ _____

Finance required for equipment — please complete the following:

Type and make of equipment and name of supplier	New/ Second hand	Price	Installation Charge	Carriage Charge	VAT	Total

Finance required for equipment ....

TOTAL FINANCE REQUIRED £ _____

8. SOURCES OF FINANCE

Private Sector

Own Resources..£ _____

Bank.. _____

Other Private Sector... _____

Total Private Sector £ _____

Public Sector

Loan/Investment ....£ _____

Grant.. _____

Other Public Sector
(Local Authority, Enterprise Allowance Scheme, etc.) .... _____

Total Public Sector £ _____

Any Other Source (specify)... _____

Total Finance Required £
(To agree with the total at 7 above) _____

Note:
Projected borrowings must show the repayment arrangement and % rate assumed together with the terms of the loan. Consider margin to cover unforeseen circumstances.

BUSINESS

PROJECTED BALANCE SHEET

		Year
	Cost	Aggregat Depreciat

FIXED ASSETS

Property .... £
Plant and machinery...
Vehicles ....
Fittings ....

| | £ | £ |

CURRENT ASSETS

Stock and work in progress .... £
Trade and sundry debtors...
Cash in bank and on hand ....

Deduct: £

CURRENT LIABILITIES

Trade and sundry creditors .... £
PAYE/NI ....
VAT ....
Bank overdraft ....

Loans ....
Hire Purchase Creditors (ie balance outstanding on HP commitments) ....

TOTAL NET ASSETS ....

Represented by:
(a) Sole Trader and Partnership
CAPITAL ACCOUNT Opening balance, or
Cash/Assets transferred to business (new businesses) ....
Profit for period...

Deduct:
Personal drawings ....

OR
(b) Limited company
SHARE CAPITAL ACCOUNT .... Authorised £ .... Issu

RESERVES...

Note:
No provision made for taxation.

Net		Year 2				Year 3	
	Cost	Aggregate Depreciation	Net	Cost	Aggregate Depreciation	Net
	£			£		
	£	£	£	£	£	£
		........................£			........................£	
		£			£	
	£			£		
		........................£			........................£	
		£			£	
		£			£	
	.................Issued shares £			.................Issued shares £		
		........................£			........................£	
		£			£	

BUSINESS

CASH FLOW STATEMENT YEAR I

	Total	1		2		3		4
		Forecast	Actual	Forecast	Actual	Forecast	Actual	Forecast
INCOME								
CASH/CHEQUES RECEIVED:								
Cash sales								
Credit sales								
Capital and/or loans introduced								
Other income								
Total £								
EXPENDITURE								
CASH/CHEQUE PAYMENTS:								
Materials/Stock/Subcontractors								
Wages								
Salaries — Administration								
Rent and rates								
Heating and lighting								
Insurances								
Postage and stationery								
Property maintenance								
Repairs to plant								
Travelling and motor expenses								
Telephone								
Audit and accountancy fees								
Advertising								
Miscellaneous expenses								
Finance charges: Bank								
Other								
Proprietors'/Directors' remuneration								
Legal/Architects' fees								
Capital expenditure								
Loan/Hire/Lease purchase repayments								
Other payments								
VAT								
Taxation								
Total £								
Movement — income less expenditure £								
Opening balance — bank £								
Closing balance — bank £								
Invoiced sales — credit £								

Month

5		6		7		8		9		10		11		12	
Forecast	Actual	Forecast	Actual	Forecast	Actual	Forecast	Actual	Forecast	Actual	Forecast	Actual	Forecast	Actual	Forecast	Actual

Sales .... £

Materials/Subcontractors .... £

Direct wages
(including National Insurance) ....

Increase/(Decrease) in stock of
materials and work in progress...... _____

GROSS PROFIT ....

Deduct:

Salaries and remuneration
(including National Insurance) .... £

Rent and rates ....

Heating and lighting.......................

Insurances ....

Postage and stationery ....

Repairs and renewals....................

Travelling and motor expenses..

Telephone ....

Professional fees............................

Advertising ....

Miscellaneous expenses ....

Finance charges ....

    Bank ....

    HP ....

    Loan ....

    Interest   ....

    Depreciation ....

    ....

    ....

    ....

    ....

    ....

    ....

Total expenses ...._____

TRADING PROFIT (LOSS) ....£

Add:

Miscellaneous income ....

NET PROFIT (LOSS) BEFORE TAX ......

Note:

Personal drawing or Directors'
remuneration included above ....£

Note:

VAT is excluded where it can be reclaimed.

BUSINESS

CASH FLOW STATEMENT YEAR 2

	Total	Quarter			
		1st	2nd	3rd	4th
INCOME					
CASH/CHEQUES RECEIVED:					
Cash sales					
Credit sales					
Capital and/or loans introduced					
Other income					
Total £					
EXPENDITURE					
CASH/CHEQUE PAYMENTS:					
Materials/Stock/Subcontractors					
Wages					
Salaries — Administration					
Rent and rates					
Heating and lighting					
Insurances					
Postage and stationery					
Property maintenance					
Repairs to plant					
Travelling and motor expenses					
Telephone					
Audit and accountancy fees					
Advertising					
Miscellaneous expenses					
Finance charges: Bank					
Other					
Proprietors'/Directors' remuneration					
Legal/Architects' fees					
Capital expenditure					
Loan/Hire/Lease purchase repayments					
Other payments					
VAT					
Taxation					
Total £					
Movement — income less expenditure £					
Opening balance — bank £					
Closing balance — bank £					
Invoiced sales — credit £					

BUSINESS

CASH FLOW STATEMENT YEAR 3

INCOME

Annual
total

CASH/CHEQUES RECEIVED:

Cash sales
Credit sales
Capital and or loans introduced
Other income

Total £

EXPENDITURE

CASH/CHEQUE PAYMENTS:

Materials/Stock/Subcontractors
Wages
Salaries –– Administration
Rent and rates
Heating and lighting
Insurances
Postage and stationery
Property maintenance
Repairs to plant
Travelling and motor expenses
Telephone
Audit and accountancy fees
Advertising
Miscellaneous expenses
Finance charges: Bank
                 Other
Proprietors'/Directors' remuneration
Legal/Architects' fees
Capital expenditure
Loan/Hire/Lease purchase repayments
Other payments
VAT
Taxation

Total £

Movement — income less expenditure £
Opening balance — bank £
Closing balance — bank £

Invoiced sales — credit £

The Man With The Money

So to recap, set out your business plan, profit forecast and cashflow forecast. Armed with these you can now approach your bank manager for his understanding and most important his financial support. You will however still have to sell your case, which is your business and you. This you should do with absolute confidence. Remember, it is the bank's job to lend you money and as long as they are certain that you are able to repay without problems they will be happy to do so. After all, that is how they make their living.

Most banks will provide a range of services including business overdrafts, small business loans of £1,000 to £15,000, business loans of £15,000 plus, property finance and business mortgages. They will usually seek some security on larger loans. If you have a house with a percentage of the mortgage paid off the part of the house that you own can be offered as security on a loan. These are big steps to take, especially when you put your home on the line. Be sure of your plans and the realistic nature of them.

Most banks nowadays will give you the first year free of bank charges if you open a business account with them. Find out what special services each bank will offer you before you place your business with them. They may even offer preferential interest rates for a business starting up. Shop around and do not take the first bank you visit as banks are very competitive these days and only too keen to offer you better terms than the one down the road.

Accounts and Your Accountant

Unless you are totally adept with the workings of the Inland Revenue it would be wise to hire the services of an accountant. Like all professionals, accountants are expensive and vary enormously in ability and commitment to their clients. It is important to find a good accountant that you can trust. The best recommendation is by word of mouth. Ask your colleagues if they are satisfied with their accountant and if they can recommend him. Make sure that the accountant specialises with the setting up of small businesses and preferably has a basic grasp of natural medicine. There is no point in approaching someone who only deals with large firms or has no understanding of your profession. Then ask the accountant for a basic scale of fees which is usually assessed by the hour. They do vary. If you are able to complete monthly accounts yourself this will minimise the accountant's fees considerably, and enable you to use his services only once a year to endorse and submit your accounts to the authorities. Check that your accountant will be helpful and is prepared to give you pointers in the setting up of your accounts.

TSB BANK – BUSINESS SERVICES FOR THE MEDICAL PROFESSIONS

ON-LINE REAL TIME COMPUTER SYSTEM

Via the TSB branch network, transactions performed over any of our branch counters throughout the country are instantly value-dated at the account holding branch.

SURGERY LOANS

Loans available at extremely competitive rates to enable practitioners to build new surgeries, improve existing premises or convert properties for surgery use under the cost rent scheme, or buy into a practice. Fixed and variable rates are available with a choice of repayment methods.

LOANS FOR COMPUTER SYSTEMS, EQUIPMENT AND FURNISHINGS

Loan facilities are available for these items.

SPEEDLINK

The TSB's telephone banking system, now available to businesses, which provides a wide range of facilities including balance enquiry, regular bill payments, transfers between accounts and transaction enquiries since last statement. The service can also be used in conjunction with customers own 'FAX' machines to link directly into the bank's computer system and provide up to the minute bank statements.

MANAGED ACCOUNT

A Business current account providing all the facilities of an ordinary account, including cheque book and full money transmission services, but with the added advantage of paying interest on cleared credit balances. Interest rates are competitive and are tiered to provide maximum benefits automatically. Instant access is available without penalty. No more time consuming transfers between accounts to maximise interest earned.

OTHER SERVICES INCLUDE:-

Trustcard, Mortgages, Personal Loans, Insurance Services, Pension Planning.

FOR FURTHER INFORMATION OR ASSISTANCE, PLEASE CONTACT YOUR NEAREST TSB COMMERCIAL BRANCH.

There are several systems available for keeping accounts. In the first instance, your accountant will advise on the system that his company is familiar with and the relevant account ledgers to buy. These can be bought from any large stationers in the high street. It is advisable to write up your accounts on at least a monthly basis, and not leave it for a year and then expect to keep track of things. You won't remember half of it and will probably end up losing essential receipts and other information. Keeping accounts is a thankless task which produces no income, so it can cause some feelings of resentment. Nevertheless they have to be done, and the more you do for yourself, the more you save on accountant's fees. Keep a regular time each week for book keeping. Once you have established the habit it will become less painful.

On the accounts ledger page you need to have two columns, one for credit and one for debit. We set out an example below:-

For an example of accounts, see page 68-69.

In the first year of trading, because of the financial outlay to buy fixtures, fittings, stock and possible repayments on a loan, this will greatly reduce your tax liabilities. You may have even made a loss on paper when your personal allowance is taken into account. This can work to your advantage as subsequent years are usually assessed on the figures for the first year of trading. It is in these delicate initial years that you need all the help you can get. You will have your tax bill deferred to the later years (year four onwards). You will not be getting away with paying tax if you make a good profit however, but at least you have some breathing space in years one to three. This is providing that you do not make too much money and that you offset profit against capital items and expenses. Offsetting profits by reinvesting in your business used to offer 100% relief on capital expenditure. Now it is only 33%. This does not exactly encourage investment these days.

Your accountant will advise you of the best period of time to choose as your accounting year. This need not coincide with the tax year. You pay tax on your taxable profits. These are your takings during the tax year. In addition, any money owed by you at the beginning of the accounting year and any money owed to you at the end of the accounting year plus any increase in the value of stock you own is taken into account and liable for tax. Deducted from this figure are: capital allowances (25% of the total cost of equipment such as computers and office equipment used exclusively and wholly for business); money owed to you at the start of the accounting year; money owed by you at the end of the accounting year; losses; half the money of any Class 4 National Insurance contributions you pay in the year of assessment; allowable business expenses.

Earning Under £10,000 A Year

A new law has been passed which helps the small business considerably. If you run a full or part-time business you would normally send the Inland Revenue

JUNE 1990

DATE	RECEIPTS	TOTAL			DATE	PAYMENTS
1 June	WORTHING CLINIC	120 00			1 June	NOMA
1 June	PORTSMOUTH "	95 00			5 June	WAGES
1 June	CHICHESTER "	175 00			5 June	SP&A Ltd
8 June	WORTHING "	115 00			8 June	CLAYMORE GARAGE
8 June	PORTSMOUTH "	110 00			8 June	INLAND REVENUE
8 June	CHICHESTER "	185 00			12 June	WAGES
15 June	WORTHING "	115 00			15 June	VEHICLE LICENCE OF
15 June	PORTSMOUTH "	150 00			19 June	WAGES
15 June	CHICHESTER "	110 00			19 June	NATURAL HEALTH Se
22 June	WORTHING "	110 00			19 June	BURTON NEWSPAPER
22 June	PORTSMOUTH "	160 00			22 June	C.N.H.C.
22 June	CHICHESTER "	190 00			26 June	RAYNER SERVICES
29 June	WORTHING "	120 00			27 June	PETTY CASH
29 June	PORTSMOUTH "	125 00			29 June	FRIENDS PORTFOLI
29 June	CHICHESTER "	140 00			30 June	POST OFFICE
					30 June	WAGES
		2020 00				

JULY 1990

DATE	RECEIPTS	TOTAL			DATE	PAYMENTS
6 July	WORTHING CLINIC	125 00			2 July	NOMA
6 July	PORTSMOUTH "	130 00			3 July	WAGES
6 July	CHICHESTER "	165 00			5 July	NATURAL HEALTH Se
13 July	WORTHING "	95 00			5 July	SOUTHERN ELECTRIC
13 July	PORTSMOUTH "	140 00			5 July	COMPUPRINT
13 July	CHICHESTER "	180 00			9 July	WAGES
20 July	WORTHING "	85 00			11 July	WAGES
20 July	PORTSMOUTH "	125 00			11 July	CASTLE COURT GARAGE
20 July	CHICHESTER "	175 00			17 July	BRITISH TELECOM
27 July	WORTHING "	110 00			17 July	WAGES
27 July	PORTSMOUTH "	100 00			20 July	C.N.H.C.
27 July	CHICHESTER "	150 00			24 July	PETTY CASH
					26 July	WAGES
					26 July	RAYNER SERVICES
					30 July	FRIENDS PORTFOLI
		1580 00			31 July	JOAN HARPER

TOTAL	STOCK/ MEDICINES	WAGES	ADVERTISING STATIONERY POSTAGE	MOTOR & PETROL EXPENSES	HEATING ELECTRICITY TELEPHONE	RENTS RATES LOANS	PETTY CASH	SUNDRIES INCLUDING EQUIPMENT
63 54	63 54							
150 00		150 00						
5 52			5 52					
24 95				24 95				
147 38								147 38
200 00		200 00						
55 00				55 00				
150 00		150 00						
31 12	31 12							
11 70			11 70					
263 84						263 84		
23 00				23 00				
10 00							10 00	
62 94								62 94
20 00			20 00					
150 00		150 00						
1368 99	94 66	650 00	37 22	102 95		263 84	10 00	210 32

TOTAL	STOCK/ MEDICINES	WAGES	ADVERTISING STATIONERY POSTAGE	MOTOR & PETROL EXPENSES	HEATING ELECTRICITY TELEPHONE	RENTS RATES LOANS	PETTY CASH	SUNDRIES INCLUDING EQUIPMENT
63 54	63 54							
150 00		150 00						
51 30	51 30							
30 58					30 58			
26 62			26 62					
50 00		50 00						
150 00		150 00						
26 10				26 10				
65 40					65 40			
150 00		150 00						
260 52						260 52		
15 00							15 00	
100 00		100 00						
24 30				24 30				
62 94								62 94
80 00						80 00		
1306 30	114 84	600 00	26 62	50 40	95 98	340 52	15 00	62 94

accounts to show how you have worked out your profits. However, from 6 April 1990 onwards, as long as your gross business takings or earnings before expenses are less than £10,000 a year, instead of sending the Inland Revenue detailed accounts, you have to fill in a form which tells them:

* your gross business takings or earnings including any commission or tips,
* your total business purchases and expenses
* your net profit.

If you might be eligible to submit these 'three line accounts', ask your tax office for further information.

Similarly, if you receive income such as rent from letting property, as long as the gross income before taking off any expenses is below £10,000 all you need to tell them is the gross income, the total amount of your allowable expenses and the net income and profits.

What You Can Claim On The Business

When keeping accounts always maintain full and clear records of everything you buy and sell. Get receipts for *everything*. Your accountant should tell you what you can claim as business expenses. This will include: raw materials used to decorate and kit out your clinics; specialised clothing used by some therapists; small tools required for maintenance and decorating work at the clinic; a proportion of car expenses which reflect business use; travelling expenses; fees paid to conference organisers and professional bodies; heating, light and telephone expenses (calculated on how much space you use if you work from home); the costs of goods bought for resale and raw materials; advertising; delivery charges; cleaning; rent of business premises; business rate; postage; stationery; design and printing costs; relevant books and publications; professional fees; bank charges on business accounts; wages, salaries, redundancies and reasonable leaving payments paid to employees; pensions paid to ex-employees and their dependents; retraining costs for employees who are leaving and training costs for employees to acquire and improve skills needed in their current job; insurance premiums for the business; entertaining of your staff; gifts up to £10 per year per person and gifts of any value to staff; overnight accommodation costs, dinner and breakfast (not lunch!) on business trips; repairs to the business property.

This is not a comprehensive list of business expenses and nor do we set out all the complexities of income tax in this book. We advise that you seek the expertise of a reputable professional and keep up to date with the tax laws which are altered at every budget. Publications such as the *Which?* guides to becoming self employed and running small businesses are clear, comprehensive and are constantly updated.

National Insurance

Another expense is National Insurance contributions if you are a self employed sole trader or in a partnership. You will have to pay a Class 2 stamp on a weekly basis. It is against the law not to do so. You can arrange to do this by direct debit or by buying the stamps in a post office. Although the sum is lower than a Pay As You Earn contribution you get very little for the privilege of contributing to the government's coffers in this way. You are only entitled to a means tested income support (social security) if you become unemployed and a means tested sickness benefit if you fall ill. Altogether, the National Insurance contributions are of little use to you unless you find yourself on the breadline and a private insurance scheme is necessary to protect yourself more fully from ill fortune. This is also expensive for self employed people. Government policies on self employment offer very little encouragement for the struggling entrepreneur.

VAT

Value Added Tax is another system that you will have to become familiar with. All businesses with a turn over exceeding £25,400 (figure correct at time of publication – subject to change with each budget) are liable to register for VAT and charge VAT on their products and services which are not zero rated (like, for instance, books which do not incur VAT at present). Remember that if you are registered for VAT on your services and products you can also claim VAT on services, products and most expenses bought in by the business. VAT returns are submitted on a monthly or quarterly basis. You can elect whether to submit them 12 times or 4 times a year, according to your preference.

If you obtain an income from the practise of natural medicine, give lectures, or retail or wholesale any products which are not regarded as foodstuffs you are liable to register for VAT if your turn over exceeds the £25,400 threshold. The VAT laws can be idiosyncratic and confusing. Products which are generally regarded as foodstuffs are sometimes liable for VAT and vice versa. Before you offer any goods or services *always* check the VAT status of your business. Failure to do so may cost you a considerable amount of money.

To simplify the rules which assess whether or not you are liable to charge VAT, in April 1990 the Chancellor of the Exchequer abolished the system which required that each business predict the quarterly and annual turn over thresholds which is a very difficult calculation in any trade or profession. Instead of consulting the crystal ball to see if you will have a turn over which exceeds the VAT threshold of £25,400, you can now look back at the actual turn over figures for the last twelve months. In others words, assessment is retrospective rather than prospective.

Another important change is that, in the past, you were liable to pay VAT on all sales, even if you had not actually received the money for them. This means that your VAT figure was calculated on all the fees owed as well as the fees paid. From April 1991, any debts over two years old (on which you have paid VAT) and written off your books, will qualify for relief from VAT. Take it from us, you will find yourself with patients who do not pay their bills. This is a less palatable aspect of human nature. They will forget their cheque books, bounce cheques and receive goods in the post from you and 'lose' the invoice. You will inevitably waste time and money attempting to recover money owed to you. Make sure you make every effort to receive payment at the time of consultation. It saves much time and bother.

To return to VAT. VAT adds a significant amount to your charges and will make you 15% more expensive than a practitioner who is not VAT registered. It is advisable to attempt to stay below the limit. This can be done by separating the sale of supplements from the consultation fees and placing them under another business name. You can bank your consultation fees under your personal name which you use in practice but have a separate set of accounts and business bank account for the sale of remedies, supplements, tonics, relaxation tapes or any other goods you may supply to your clients. Call it 'Supplementary Benefits'! Any name will do, as long as you completely separate fees and goods in all ways.

There are ways in which you can split your practices if the consultation fees earned from your clinics go over the £25,400 threshold. These will enable you to stay below the £25,400 limit and are not complicated but they can be questioned by the Customs and Excise authorities. It is essential to set up and register separate clinics with the guidance of a reputable accountant to ensure that your system is watertight and above board.

We cannot state too strongly that you must obtain sound advice from a reputable professional before establishing any such scheme to divide your businesses. It is very easy to miss a detail or misunderstand a way of managing finance and find that you are in fact eligible for VAT and that you do not have the resources to pay your debt. You are a professional. Do not scrimp on professional advice that can save you thousands of pounds. If it is faulty you can ignore it. Consult your accountant, solicitor, the manager and the area business manager at your bank where appropriate. Ignorance can jeopardise the entire success of your business.

What Are You Worth?

Fundamental to your business plan, cashflow predictions, banking arrangements and setting up of accounts is the thorny question of charging professional fees. As we mentioned in Chapter 1, it is all too easy to negate your financial worth. You may regard your healing abilities as a gift and a part of you feels you should not be charging but giving of yourself for nothing. Do not fall into this trap. If you undervalue your services you are saying, 'I am not worth a full fee. I am second rate'. If you are the sort of person who feels deeply uncomfortable taking money after a consultation, the solution is to hire a receptionist to deal with this side of your business. This way you separate money from healing. By employing a receptionist to do this job, she will pay for herself very quickly. She will prevent you from falling into the temptation of reducing your charges all the time. This is a very easy thing to do. You sit and hear tales of hardship and woe from a patient during an interview. An aspect of this can often be financial. The consultation comes to an end and you have to extract money. It is embarrassing and uncomfortable if you fumble it. So give the job to someone else. Separate healing from money.

We live in a world which values worth in terms of cost. Money is a totally abstract commodity. It is meant to relate to a reserve of gold hidden in a country under elaborate lock and key. This in turn is just lumps of shiny metal which is uncommon and attractive to look at but basically not particularly useful. Yet the whole world runs on it. Money is the benchmark of what is good. If something is expensive it is exclusive, sought after and valuable. If it costs little it is 'cheap and nasty'. If you do not charge for your services or undercharge, you undervalue what you are offering. You are unconsciously admitting that you are not worth the rate which other practitioners charge. Of course, if you can afford to be philanthropic and you are sitting on a private income that is marvellous. The reality for most of us is that we have bills to pay and mortgages to finance. Philanthropy is a distant ideal in most cases.

To set your consultation fees, work out exactly how much it costs you to run your clinic(s) each week. Then work out all your outgoings as you have done for your cashflow. Estimate how much you need to live on. That is your most basic amount. Realistically assess how many patients you are likely to see in a week. Divide that number by the total sum needed to pay all your bills and expenses. Are you charging enough? Is your practice a viable concern?

You may want to find out what other practitioners are charging. Phone them up and find out their fees. Obviously, therapists in London have to charge far more than therapists in the provinces because their overheads are so high. Practitioners with busy clinics and well established reputations are also able to charge more than younger, less well known ones. Fees vary from £20 an hour to upwards of £50 per hour. You may also like to structure your fees so that students, OAPs and children qualify for reduced rates. Homeopaths, chiropractors and acupuncturists usually charge less for follow up appointments which take up less consultation time. Research this field and fix your prices with those in the area and according to your needs. Remember, if you are too cheap you do yourself a disservice. You will not stay in practice if you cannot meet your financial commitments. If you sort out the sticky problem of money, you are more likely to practise with a clear mind and ultimately you will be a better therapist.

Chapter 8

SELLING YOUR WARES

Effective marketing and PR. Word of mouth. Business cards. Letter head. Image. Printing and printers. Brass and other kinds of plaque. Getting known: free PR. Lectures. Organisations to approach. Addresses. Advertising. Local newspapers. Magazines. Writing sales copy and advertisments. The 'AIDA' principle. Yellow Pages. Teaching courses. Adult Education courses. Using Direct Mail. Using computers and word processors.

So now you have qualified in your chosen field, set up your clinic in the place of your choice and are ready to start the real work. Where do your patients/clients materialise from? No doubt your friends have heard all about your endeavours and have possibly had the privilege of being your first guinea pigs. They will be of great assistance to you in the early days by spreading the word of your skills and your location. Never underestimate the power of the grapevine. It is far more valuable than countless newspaper advertisements because of its *personal* nature. People are more willing to trust a good word in their ear than all the glossy ads in the world. They feel that they are less likely to be conned this way. Of course, one good word leads to another and soon your patients will be singing your praises to their friends. The circle will expand and more and more people will come to you.

If you are naturally retiring and avoid social situations, this is the time to cast away your shyness and get out there! Tell people what you are doing and communicate your enthusiasm for your profession. Your positive outlook will be magnetic. We are not suggesting, however, that you become a dreadful bore, eyeballing all and sundry and trapping them in endless monologues about natural medicine. Just chat to the receptive. Our experience is that people will want to talk to you and will be very interested in what you are doing. You are different and your training is unusual. Some will probably want to tell you in great detail about their ailments. When you are successful you may find yourself keeping quiet about your work to avoid this!

To this day, we find grateful patients from long ago still recommending us to their friends and associates. This is the best form of advertising and, strangely enough, clients who come to us through the personal grapevine often seem to respond the best to treatment. It is as though the trust and positive reputation invested in us starts to work before the person steps through our doors. They believe that we are able to cure them and this, in itself, has a placebo effect before the treatment itself has even begun. If you are able to attract this sort of response your job as a therapist will be far easier. You will spend less time winning trust and respect. Of course, the therapy is essential to this. You cannot survive on your positive outlook alone!

There are various approaches to building up a patient list and not all of them have to be shatteringly expensive. Firstly, you must have a business card showing your name and qualifications, your services and the addresses and telephone numbers of your clinics. Spend time looking at the design and layout of other cards from all professions and then design your card to suit your needs. You may want a simple black on white card with a minimum of information or you may want a logo and colours. Obviously, the simpler the card the cheaper it is to produce but depending on your field of work, an unusual logo and card may attract custom. Only you can assess the value of the image you need.

Printing

If you choose the type-face and basically design the card yourself you will also save money. It need not be a complicated procedure and your printer will help. You will probably need a letter head and 'With Compliments' slips, especially if you are sending out remedies, essential oils and the like. Design each of these at the same time to complement each other. Using the same logo, colours, paper, etc. for each is not only cheaper, it also helps affirm the image you wish to convey and makes you more memorable. Give consideration to the impression you wish to make as this is a world of image and small touches do add to your professionalism. However, we know that professionalism is not the car you drive or the card you offer and that these are shallow benchmarks. We are just suggesting that they help establish the practitioner. People will remember you and keep your card, especially if it stands out.

Printers vary enormously in price. We recently had estimates for compliments slips, business cards, fax forms and letter heads. All of these were already designed and we required a quality job on quality paper. One estimate was for £634. An estimate from the same company but obtained by an associate of that company was for £340. Another printer was charging £230 and a further printer offered to do the work for £194. We were concerned with the quality of work from the last printer whom we did not know so we went back to the £230 quote whose work had proved satisfactory in the past and told him of the more competitive figure. He agreed to match the £194 price but we agreed to wait a week so that he could run it through at a convenient time to him when his printing machine was already inked for some other job with the same colour that we required. The quality was excellent and so was the price. He was happy to do the job, being a small firm, and we were happy to save money but retain quality.

Besides business cards it is also a good idea to place a plaque outside your clinic announcing your presence to the world. The conventional plaque is made of brass and will cost roughly £50 - £80. However, you may want to buy a white plastic sign with black or blue lettering. (They are not so bad as they sound and can look smart!) Again, they are fairly expensive. Another option is to use a piece of oak with bevelled edges, letraset it yourself and seal it with yacht varnish. This looks very presentable and is significantly less expensive.

Getting Known: Free PR

Now all your friends and associates know of your work, the printing is collected and your sign is outside the clinic, what do you do? First, you need to explore all avenues of advertising that are free. Go to all the health food shops in the area and introduce yourself. Ask them if you can put up a card on their wall or board. Ask them if you could possibly leave a pile of cards, or better still, leaflets explaining what you do for enquirers. These are invaluable contacts as they are sympathetic to natural medicine and they know you will recommend a healthy diet and possibly vitamins, minerals and tonics as part of your therapy. Let them know that your services complement theirs and that you both will mutually benefit from your association. Make friends. The best thing you can do is be a customer as well. Practise what you preach.

Visit all the health clubs in the area, introduce yourself and leave a card or a leaflet. Offer to give talks on natural medicine. There is nothing like a captive audience. Gymnasiums and sports centres are also worth a visit, especially for chiropractors, osteopaths and for hypnotherapists specialising in increasing sports potential. Also, introduce yourself to your local chemist. He or she would welcome an authoritative source to direct queries regarding natural medicine.

You may also want to write a letter to all the general practitioners in the area informing them of your services, fees and whereabouts and enclosing a card for their waiting room wall. You will be surprised by the sympathetic responses you will get. Many GPs are open minded, especially about counselling, psychotherapy, hypnotherapy and the manipulative therapies. They can only offer drugs for psychological complaints and do not have the time themselves to counsel their patients. Complaints like back pain are dealt with by drugs and rest. They may welcome the services of an osteopath or chiropractor. Many patients have come to us from GPs and still do. Do not be surprised by the more old fashioned, negative response, but, despite the occasional charge of quackery, our experience has shown that it is worth contacting GPs.

Some practitioners write to their patients' GP and inform him of their prescription if any usual findings are present. This helps the GP to develop an understanding of what the practitioner is doing and why. Obviously, this course is appropriate to some disciplines and not to others. We are aware that some patients do not wish their GP to know that they are seeking the skills of a natural medical practitioner. You can only assess the value of this action by your own experience but it is worth considering.

It is also worth letting other natural practitioners in the area know that you are there. They may be able to recommend you to people requiring your discipline. Go and see whoever will see you and have a chat. Personal contacts are invaluable. You are more likely to meet with a positive response by putting a face to a name.

Another form of public relations is to contact groups in your area and offer to lecture on your chosen discipline. Groups welcome speakers and often offer a fee, especially if you speak well and entertain. Women's Institutes, Mother's Unions, National Childbirth Trust, Rotary and Lions clubs are an obvious choice. There may be groups at your local hospital who are interested such as the Back Pain Association and asthma or arthritis groups. There are many groups who also require after dinner speakers. A trip to your local library is worthwhile. They will have the contact names and addresses of groups in the area. The main aim is to get your name known. You will be surprised how many clients come to you through these free sources. You will be especially welcome if you can approach your subject from an interesting angle. Follow-up invitations will also come from other groups if you go down well.

The following few pages relate primarily to advertising and we appreciate that some natural practitioners are restricted by the regulations set out by their professional bodies. We recommend that you read them even if you feel that they do not apply to you as a number of ideas are presented that apply generally to all forms of marketing.

Advertising

Newspaper advertising is expensive. Some practitioners do place advertisements for their premises and services in the personal columns of local papers. This can be effective. Make sure that your advertising copy is brief, to the point and interesting. If the first sentence catches the eye you are likely to receive enquiries. If you advertise regularly you should be able to negotiate a reduced rate with the paper. Remember that *everything* is negotiable.

Advertising revenue is a vital part of a newspaper's income. A free paper is usually entirely dependent upon it. Papers need to sell advertising space and so do the space salesmen to earn their wages. They often reduce their rates substantially if you are prepared to haggle hard enough, particularly the free papers. Don't spend any more than is necessary. The papers will have a discount margin available if you are prepared to squeeze them for it. Why should *they* take any more of your hard earned money than is necessary? You need what you can save more than they do. Be a good and fair therapist to your patients, but when it comes to suppliers, advertising salesmen etc., it is everyone for themselves. That is business in this day and age. Without a little bit of that attitude you could find yourself devoured by the predators in what is a very dense and dangerous jungle. We are, of course, not suggesting that you act unscrupulously or without ethics. You can be sharp and astute without being bent.

Back to the papers. There is a logical line of thought that because the free papers are free, they are usually delivered unsolicited. As such, they often find their way post haste into the dustbin or to light the fire without so much as a cursory glance. However, the free papers in particular are usually hungry for news, any news, because generally they lack any! It is very likely that if you present your new clinic, exhibition, course or whatever as a 'news item', it will be snapped up with relish. Any publicity is worthwhile, however limited, especially if it is free.

Should you decide, for whatever reason, to advertise in a free paper or any paper, magazine or other publication, it is essential to monitor the results. You need to calculate if the advertisement has paid for itself. This can be done by including a coded cut out coupon in the advertisement perhaps or, more simply (and less accurately), just by asking new patients where they heard about your clinic. Monitoring, at least to give you a rough idea, is important as it is easy to throw good money away on advertisements or publications that do not work. If you do not monitor the situation, you will never have a clear picture of what is working and what is not. If you find your advertisement has not worked it is likely to be because it was not effective (try a different version), the publication was not appropriate for your target audience, timing (wrong time of year, e.g. everyone on holiday or too busy preparing for Christmas) or some other reason. If you analyse the results you have a chance of getting it right next time or improving on the success you did have.

Papers and magazines often have some space left just before publication which they are dying to fill. If you let a salesman know that you may be interested in buying cheap, just before publication space, doubtless when the situation occurs you will receive a call from him. A case in point was a publishing friend who was called by a national newspaper late on a Friday afternoon selling cheap space for the Monday edition. An advertisement that was worth £300 was being offered for £150. It was obvious that they did not want the paper to go to press with blank spaces in it, so he offered them £50. After a certain amount of eager debate (the salesman was keen to finish his sales and start his weekend), our friend, having stuck to his guns, told them to take the £50 or leave it. Sure enough, on the Monday, the advertisement appeared in the paper. This happened three times in two months. Our friend received £900 worth of advertising in a national newspaper for just £150. **Everything is negotitable.**

When writing an advertisement you need to attract the reader immediately as you will often be competing with many other advertisements for his attention. The position of it can help. At the right hand side of a right hand page, as near to the front of the publication as possible is a good rule of thumb (on the front even better, but probably expensive). As one turns the page this is the first part of a new page to be seen. Having placed your advertisement in a good position (which might cost a little extra) you now have to make the reader read your advertisement rather than anything else on the page.

The general direct marketing principle of 'AIDA' is a good one to follow when writing copy for advertisements, leaflets, letters or anything where you want people to pay attention to what you have to say. AIDA stands for Attention, Interest, Desire, Action. The first thing you have to do is to make the reader stop in his tracks and pay *Attention*. This can be done using an appropriate headline and perhaps sub headline:

You *have won a holiday for two*
in Bermuda.
No strings attached!

If even the most obvious direct mailing piece came through your letterbox with a message like that, it would be hard to ignore. You would at least be tempted to read on to find out what the catch actually was! Obviously you are not going to be offering free holidays, but the point is to make the personal ('you') benefit to the reader as strong, persuasive and unstoppably eye-catching as truth and your creative ability can manage. Next, you need to increase his *Interest* by telling the reader more about what you are offering. Then introduce the *Desire* factor: why what you have to offer is just the thing the reader needs to solve his problems. Then at the end you need to make the reader *Act*. Immediately preferably, as the longer it is left the less likely he will be to do anything. You could perhaps include an incentive with a cut off deadline to inspire him into action:

Phone Now. Every enquirer booking
an appointment before 1st May
will receive the first consultation
absolutely FREE!

At all times, keep the reader's motivation to respond in mind by clearly defining the benefits he will receive. By the way, it is generally considered that free offers, money back guarantees and other incentives which you might think would encourage abuse by the customer actually increase response/sales dramatically. Abuse does occasionally happen of course, but the improved results generally make this irrelevant.

A word of warning: although the following is completely obvious, it is worth mentioning. Always remember to include your name, address and telephone number in *any* marketing that you do whether it be an advertisement, leaflet, letter, business card or whatever. Such an omission does happen to even the most professional, but usually only once! It is a foolish mistake that renders the cleverest copy writing and expenditure completely worthless as your prospective customers do not know how to find you.

We have used only the crudest of examples here to give you the impression of what is needed. Obviously a subtle, clever and even witty approach to presenting your services will probably prove the best course of action. We have also only given you the slightest outline of some of the basic direct marketing ideas. We strongly recommend that to maximise the potential of your advertising and PR campaign you read one of the standard classics on the subject, *Commonsense Direct Marketing* by Drayton Bird, published by Kogan Page. It is amusingly written and is easy to read being pleasingly free of 'Marketing Speak'.

Remember that some colleges and societies do not allow this form of advertising or strictly curtail what you may say. For example, homeopaths and acupuncturists may only place an opening announcement of the premises in the paper and other disciplines only allow the merest details like a name, profession and location. Check with your college.

Another way of using local newspapers is to come to an arrangement with them. Say, for instance, you are setting up in practice. Invite a journalist to do a feature on you and have an interesting angle thought out to tempt them. They may require that you take a box advertisement on the same page. They may not. Local papers, as we have said, are always looking for news and are usually happy to cover the opening of a new clinic or an interesting story. Do not be afraid to be pushy. They are!

An important form of advertising is the *Yellow Pages*. There are two basic types of advertising; creative advertising, such as television, newspapers and radio which alerts people to products and services, and directive advertising. Directive advertising is used when people have already made a decision to buy a product or service and are looking for somewhere to buy it from. In this way, directive complements creative advertising and reinforces the message. *Yellow Pages* is the number one directive advertising medium.

Yellow Pages works for all types of businesses and will generate enquiries for you. Statistics prove the point. There are more than 84 million users of *Yellow Pages* per month in the United Kingdom. At least 48.5% of all adults in Great Britain have used *Yellow Pages* at least once in the last four weeks. We have found that *Yellow Pages* does pay for itself and that it is a worthwhile investment.

A successful form of PR and revenue for practitioners like homeopaths is to write and run their own first aid courses at their clinics. This introduces basic homeopathy to the public, creates an opening for retailing simple remedies and spreads the word about the practitioner. Similarly, an aromatherapist or reflexologist can run a basic introduction course on their subject. Hypnotherapists can run relaxation courses. Psychotherapists can run stress management courses for the public and for businesses. Practitioners of neurolinguistic programming can teach people with learning difficulties, public speaking or run workshops. Yoga and relaxation classes for pregnant women are also worth considering as are specialised courses in child health care. Whatever you do has an application in the workshop scenario. If you do not have enough patients, start designing and writing a course and promote it as you would your practice. It is also useful to join with other practitioners and offer a variety of expertise and subjects.

Adult education centres are a very useful way of running courses. Get in touch with your local college head and ask him or her if there is an opening for you. The advantage of working inside the adult education system is that they are responsible for advertising the courses and finding suitable locations. They are often very helpful with visual aids as well. You will find that if you have a flair for teaching, courses will be offered to you all over your area. You can also pick up teaching skills by doing the basic adult education teaching course. This gives a good grounding in modern approaches to teaching adults and helps to make your classes more dynamic and interesting.

If you have a patient list at your fingertips, either because you have bought a clinic or because your new colleagues are willing to share theirs, you can send out a mailshot. A simple direct mail campaign to patient lists, GPs and other practitioners would be likely to yield response. The GPO used to offer new businesses on the enterprise allowance scheme one thousand second class letters franked for free. Unfortunately, this scheme is at present not available.

You can either use the leaflet your college/association provides or you can design your own. A standard letter photocopied, or better, printed should accompany the leaflet. The text should follow the 'AIDA' principle and be 'you' orientated, clearly stating the benefit the reader ('you') will gain from using your services. Personalise the letter as much as possible to make it friendly; if you are only sending out a few dozen or so, it would be worth the effort to hand write the salutation, with a name if possible, i.e. 'Dear Dr Jones'. Likewise your signature and a P.S.. Postscripts are irresistible reading (say direct marketing experts) and should inspire the reader to 'ACT NOW!' having reached the end of your letter. If your letter is printed, it could be printed in two colours, black for the main body of text and blue perhaps, for a hand written salutation (even if it only says 'Dear Sir'), signature and P.S.. If you give the printer your hand written sample of these in black pen he will be able to reproduce them in any colour you want. Personalise the letter as much as you can, it has been proved to help the message to be read. You can offer incentives or discounts, this also has been proved to increase response. Perhaps include a voucher offering a 25% discount off the reader's first visit to your clinic or maybe a free initial consultation.

Direct mail is being used more and more, because essentially it works and is a profitable way of marketing (despite what you may think when you bin the 'junk mail' that comes through your letterbox!). The important thing is that you do not waste money promoting yourself blindly; with direct mail you can target more precisely, particularly in the natural medicine professions, the people who are

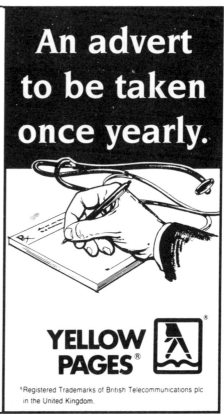

most likely to be interested in what you have to offer by using existing patient lists and so on.

A good yield for a mailshot is around a 2% response. This would be 20 new patients per 1000 letters sent. In our experience our initial mailshot yielded double that and responses continued to be received in dribs and drabs for several years. It easily paid for itself. We can only give you the merest outline of direct mailing principles here. Should this area of marketing interest you, we recommend you read, as already mentioned earlier in this chapter, *Commonsense Direct Marketing*. If you have a large patient list(s) available and are likely to do even more than just a small one-off mailshot, it is imperative reading. As with all forms of marketing, it is possible to waste a lot of money as well as make it with direct mail if you do not approach the subject with common sense and caution.

Worth mentioning here is the advantage of having a computer which can print out repeat labels for your subsequent mailshots. Once you have typed in all the addresses they are there for any future letter. With a mail merge programme, you can also personalise each letter. In fact a computer is an invaluable business tool. You can word process all your letters, write articles and leaflets and enter your accounts on to it. A computer will save you hours and you may discover a talent for writing as a word processor makes the task simple, even enjoyable and allows your creative flair to flow more easily.

Finally, if you have a flair for writing you may find that your local 'freebie' newspaper would like a regular column from you about natural medicine. We wrote one once a month for a free paper in a column called 'Alternatively Yours'. Each month a different topic in the natural medicine field was covered and we ended each article with details of our qualifications and clinics. This was an excellent way to publicise our work and a good source of patients. Furthermore, it did not cost a penny.

Chapter 9

THE SECRET WAY TO SUCCESS

Believing in yourself. Confidence. Self assessment. Positivity and other techniques. Goal setting. Imagery. Visualisation. Creating your future. Esoteric PR.

All the excellent healing ability and PR in the world will not yield the results you desire without one simple factor - believing in yourself. If you do not think you will be successful, the odds are that you will not. You will emanate that tell-tale lack of confidence to your clients and they will consciously or unconsciously pick up on it. If you believe in yourself and your abilities and you have the strong foundation of good training and an understanding of your subject you will succeed. A positive outlook is a magnet that draws people towards you. A very successful man of our acquaintance once said, "Every morning I wake up and think, 'Something remarkable is going to happen to me today,' and I am rarely disappointed." His life demonstrated his philosophy. On the other hand, if you wake up and expect disaster, the chances are that it will befall you.

Unfortunately, we are not all blessed with innate self confidence and an overflowing positive outlook. We are usually tainted by self doubts and worries. Every practitioner is concerned by the sense of responsibility involved in healing people and trying to solve their problems. Psychotherapists worry that their depressive patients may 'go over the edge' and commit suicide. Homeopaths worry about bad reactions to their remedies. Acupuncturists feel concerned about unlocking a multitude of mental 'sins' when they treat a person who ostensibly only comes to them with a physical ailment. Chiropractors worry about using the wrong manipulative approach to a problem. Herbalists may worry about prescribing the wrong medicinal herb. These concerns usually surface in the middle of the night!

For newly qualified practitioners who do not have the benefit of a history of their successes, these feelings can be particularly strong. During the period of study in your chosen field you have not only been learning skills to equip you in your profession, you have also been gradually letting go of your previous self. Perhaps you were a nurse, engineer, student, secretary, mother, doctor or sales representative? By the time you graduate you will have to wear a completely new mantle for the first time.

You will have had your time as a student sitting in with practising professionals and now you are sitting in your own clinic behind your desk waiting for your first 'official' patient! It is very easy at this point to hope secretly that he or she will not turn up. Do not allow this negative state of mind to prevail. Take a homeopathic remedy like Argentum Nitrum or Lycopodium, or a Bach Flower Remedy such as Rescue Remedy. Practise some well chosen relaxation techniques or do whatever you do in these stressful times. Remember that your patients are going to be more shy of you than you are of them. You will soon find out that your early patients will probably be the easiest and most pleasant to treat and that they will probably stay in touch with you for years to come.

There is no doubt that in the early stages you will have time between patients. Use that time to study, to practise visualisation and better yourself in some way. We have found, from personal experience, that the practice of visualisation, creating positive desired images of the future in the mind always works and we outline some techniques over the next few pages. People always came in to enquire and book appointments after we had sat down and worked at it. It is also a good practice to bunch all your patients' appointments together. This will make you appear busy and every one likes a success. It will provide you with periods of time in the day for study, administration and visualisation.

Because natural therapies are linked so closely with universal goodwill, therapists are unique when compared to other business professionals. The ordinary business has a product or idea which is marketed and sold. The public is persuaded that it needs this product, regardless of whether it does or not. Depending on the market and the sales techniques, the business will sink or swim.

You, however, have joined a unique club which, to an extent, works outside the persuasive mechanism of supply and demand because there is always sickness and need. The art of healing is as old as humanity itself. Because each therapy has a basic philosophical structure with tried and tested principles, visualisation, the art of mentally creating a desired positive future in your mind, is the most natural tool which works hand in hand with the goodwill, hope and harmony provided by the natural therapies. Natural therapists are caring individuals who have taken the time to explore, learn and utilise nature's resources. You have a deep fundamental wish to heal the sick and promote good health. For your service, you will be rewarded mentally, emotionally and physically.

Each one of us is an agent for our particular therapy and we know that we provide the right scenario for the patient to heal him/herself. Whatever we may believe in, we all want to give back, through our skills, to humanity at large. If you remain positive, mentally strong and healthy yourself, you will not drown or flounder in a sea of misunderstood, misused or false diffidence and humility.

ℬach Flower Remedies®

a simple and natural method of establishing equilibrium and harmony through the personality by means of non-poisonous wild flowers, discovered by Edward Bach, MB., BS., MRCS., L.R.C.P., DPH.

The Bach Remedies — established in 1936 — act as a form of supportive therapy, and having proved themselves in this form for an unblemished 50 years or more (not a word of complaint ever of any consequence), they are now in great demand throughout the world as a non-medicinal adjunct to various forms of treatments (including Allopathy). They are therefore an integral part of the whole healing spectrum, not as an alternative or interfering vehicle, but as a very respected complement to many restorative treatments and therapies.

We are often called upon by doctors (GPs included), Veterinarians, Dentists, manipulative specialists, psycho-therapists and so on, to supply the Remedies either for use within their particular service, or direct to their clients for whom the Bach Remedies, in their opinion, would prove to be beneficial. We provide this service unsolicited — therapists learn the value of the Remedies mainly through favourable word-of-mouth recommendation, and so in turn, send to us for further details, and after initial trial, find that the Remedies work in their own quiet way, as harmless, non-addictive, non-side effect support to a particular aspect of their treatment that normally would not be considered in their standard diagnosis, e.g. subservience, hatred, envy, jealousy, self recrimination, guilt, arrogance, intolerance, impatience, procrastination, lack of confidence, as well as rigidity of thought, autocratic outlook and behaviour, pride, apathy, embitterment with one's 'lot in life' (self pity), apprehension, possessiveness, feeling of despair and various forms of fears etc. They are benign in their action and result in no unpleasant reactions. They can be taken by persons of all ages, and have proved to be very effective for animals and plant life.

N.B. Genuine Bach Flower Remedies will bear the title *ℬach* Flower Remedies®, therefore please beware of dilutions, facsimiles and replicas that purport to be *"equal to"* or *"the same as"* or with any claimed association to Dr. Bach's discoveries and method of preparation — such products are **not Bach Flower Remedies.**

Further information can be obtained from:
The Bach Centre, Mount Vernon, Sotwell, Wallingford, Oxon. OX10 0PZ.
(SAE would be appreciated).

Self Assessment

Ask yourself how you see yourself. Are you the therapist that you want to be? Is this picture coloured by bits of what you were and the role you were playing before? If this is so, start changing it. Take a pen and paper and write down how you would like to see yourself. Use four headings:

Spiritually	*Mentally*	*Emotionally*	*Physically*
satisfied	understanding	happy	fit
fulfilled	patient	joyful	strong
learning	caring	able to express	glowing
exploring	open	emotions as they arise without inhibition or regret	healthy

How do I approach my professional life? Ask yourself the following questions and any others that you can think of that may be pertinent. Be realistic about yourself.

Honesty	–	do my patients get my full attention and time?
Organisation	–	are my notes and case histories up to date and correctly maintained?
Calm and cheerfulness	–	do I share this with others?
Industrious	–	do I target daily goals and achieve them?
Creativity	–	do I think of ways of improving tasks?
Planning	–	are my appointments planned? Do I organise for the future?
Self Improvement	–	am I aware of myself and do I seek to change and improve those areas that require it?
Punctuality	–	do I keep people waiting?
Reliability	–	do I do what I say I will do?
Positive thinking	–	do I believe in 'me'?

If you have any problems, it is a good idea to clarify them by writing them down. Provide a column with the solution if you have it or solutions if you have too many and are not sure which way to go. Write another column for any action to be followed or action already taken. Then forget it and relook at the paper:
* daily – until it is solved if the problem is minor
* weekly or
* monthly – depending on the size of the problem.
Readjust the columns each time. You will soon find the answer.

Setting your Goals

So what can you do about the human frailties of lack of confidence and self doubt? First of all it is a good idea to clarify what you want to get out of life. Do you want to be extremely busy, well known with media commitments as well as a stream of clients beating a path to your door? Do you want to concentrate on training others and teaching courses? Or do you want a quieter life with an adequate flow of patients and time to study further?

Ask yourself exactly where you are going and then sit down with a blank piece of paper. Begin by setting out your short-term goals. What do you want to realistically achieve in the next year professionally? Consider all aspects of your business and write down the goals in one column. Then write down your personal goals for the next year. It is important to tie in professional and personal goals. It is no good working yourself into the ground and wrecking your marriage, for instance. A healthy personal life is a foundation from which to work. We know of very few practitioners who are able to cope with the rigours of healing when their lives are in chaos. Do, however, separate personal improvement from material gain.

Goal setting is a good exercise of adventure. The world is your oyster. Whatever you want awaits you. Create it all on paper and work towards it daily, weekly, monthly and annually. Write your goals in your favourite bright coloured felt tip pens and learn to visualise the shape, smell, variety, colour and feel of what you want. These goals are seedlings that need nursing daily. Rearrange them as you progress, if necessary. Do not just write down your goals and leave them in a dark drawer. You need to remind yourself of where you are going and what you are doing. This method prevents your life from slipping away in a blur leaving you wondering where the last five, ten or fifteen years have gone. There will always be those goals standing like milestones for you to look back on and say, 'I've accomplished them!'

Keep your old goals somewhere when you have superseded them. We recently reviewed our long and short-term goals written down in 1988. To our gratification, we had achieved all of the short-term goals and all but one of the long-term goals within two years. At the time of writing, our goals had seemed elusive dreams. They came true. Realising we had achieved them was a tremendous boost to our confidence.

When you have fully considered your strategy for the next year, write down your long-term goals in the same way. Give yourself a realistic time span so that these plans are not nebulous. It is a good idea to set your goals with your spouse and your business partner. You may find a few surprises. Choose a time when you will not be interrupted. Go out if you have to and make goal setting a special and enjoyable occasion. Involving your partner in your plans and ambitions is enormously positive. It also helps you to crystallise those dreams and ideas which lurk in the back of your mind.

Creating Your Future

Once you have clearly established what you want and where you are going, it is time to start creating that future in your mind. This is the basis of visualisation.

Find a quiet place where you are unlikely to be disturbed and go through a standard relaxation routine which suits you. If you have self hypnosis techniques to draw upon, all the better. Once you have achieved a state of relaxation begin to create the future in your mind in a year's time. You may relate better to sounds than to clear images. You may be able to access feelings best of all or even smells. You may be lucky and be able to do all four. Whatever your abilities your aim is to create a scenario in your mind in the most persuasive and realistic manner possible.

For example, visualise your appointment book being full of names. See patients coming to your clinics and you welcoming them. See them in consultation looking happy and relaxed. See them shaking your hand with gratitude because you have been able to help them. Create pictures of yourself in the successful situations which you have set as your goals. These may be teaching classes; giving interesting lectures to responsive audiences; giving interviews on the radio and to papers; studying and understanding problems involved with your therapy; making housecalls; and finally, going to the bank and having a healthy financial outlook! Make these pictures as real as possible. Fill them in with details. Give them colour, dimension and make stories with them like a film if you can.

You may be a person who cannot happily create pictures but can experience sensations, feel emotions, imagine smells and hear sounds. Whatever your ability, create the future in yourself. Hear the bell ringing at your clinic and the door opening. Hear the footsteps in the hall, the welcoming sounds, the appreciation at your successful treatment, the clapping at your lectures, the interest in the questions asked. Feel the sense of achievement success brings, the confidence and security at being able to pay your bills, the experience of being busy with many appointments, the sense of satisfaction at giving good talks and being a sought after therapist. You may even want to imagine the taste or smells of your favourite but fabulously expensive dinner and imagine yourself sitting down in a relaxed and happy social situation to eat this feast which you could not afford without a modicum of success!

Whatever your skills, use them to create positive images, sounds, feelings and even smells. Remember your abilities and strengths at these sessions and tell yourself every day that you are competent, successful, confident and committed to your goals and the well-being of your clients in your chosen discipline. Practise this mental approach every day. Reality is a matter of energy. If you create your success on the faster mental level you are beginning a process which crystallises the prospect in the slower physical world we inhabit. It is time and hard work which brings the rewards but these are infinitely more attainable if they already clearly exist in your mind. If you believe you can do it you will. All human achievement starts first with a thought.

Chapter 10

PROFILE OF A PRACTITIONER

Image and appearance. What type of practitioner are you? The importance of mixing with other practitioners. Beware of gurus.

The image of the practitioner is an all important aspect. It is the manner in which you relate to and are seen by your patients. Some practitioners are more at home dressing in a more casual style and having a relaxed, laid back approach to their therapy. Whereas others will dress in a three piece suit and have a more formal approach. And others, because of practical reasons, will wear a white coat or overall. Whatever style of dress you adopt, you should always be aware that first impressions are high on the list for new patients.

The image you project will be based on your conception of what a practitioner is. This will vary from person to person. The vicinity in which you practise, whether in the city or in the country, may influence the image you adopt. We would, however, emphasise that people have come to expect a certain approach, largely due to the orthodox medical profession, which may alarm some patients if you deviate too much from it. The patients have to have confidence in the way in which you present yourself. This enables them to relax in your company and allows them to express their symptoms, especially their innermost emotions. The emotional responses of the patients are important and every step should be taken to allow patients to express these freely.

The ability to listen does not come naturally to everyone. In the beginning, most practitioners will have to be consciously aware of their input into the consultation and to interject only at times when the patient wanders off the relevant train of thought, pertaining to their illness. A knowledge of your therapy, a caring attitude, attentiveness, openness, thoroughness, punctuality and a genuine desire to heal the sick are qualities to strive for. Excessive concern with the image you project is not healthy and acts as an obstruction in therapy.

However well you practise or prescribe, you will not be able to cure everyone, and you will inevitably have your failures, which you will hopefully recognise and refer to other practitioners. With most natural therapies the need for on-going study is a must. Keep abreast with new information, changing trends and any literature on your particular therapy and others. The effort and discipline required will pay dividends in the long-term.

To acquaint yourself with the philosophy of your chosen subject will stimulate and enthuse, as very often it stems from ancient cultures and traditions which contain true wisdom that time will never forget and modern legislation cannot destroy. Such philosophies can be a guideline by which to live your own life, or a pathway to follow, if you want to.

What sort of therapist are you? Do you wear a white coat and work in an apparently sterile, clinical environment? Are you very familiar with your patients, like a friend, dressing casually and more likely to become emotionally involved in your cases? Are you very detached and cold? Are you extremely formal in business suit, sitting behind a large desk? To a certain extent you work with an image that is most comfortable but do beware of extremes if you want to succeed with most patients who encounter you. We do not have to take extremes on board and it is wiser not to. Every practitioner seeks balance. He must be a real person but remain professional. Distance is not a bad quality. Coldness with a lack of empathy is. Finding the balance is difficult and is usually achieved with time and by making mistakes.

It is always good to meet and mix with fellow practitioners, socially and professionally. You can share in your common interests and be supportive to one another in times of need. In our multi-therapy natural health centre, we organised monthly meetings with fellow practitioners and each month a chosen practitioner would have the opportunity to present one of his most difficult cases. After presenting his case, each therapist in turn could ask questions and make suggestions. We found this very useful and rewarding as it opened up different ways to approach the case in question. Important also is the fact that you can get to know each other better and create a feeling of unity, working together towards common goals. This we believe is important as one can so easily become isolated in one's own therapy. Mixing with other practitioners at work or socially is a good way to maintain communication with people of like mind. We all have friends outside our work environment which is very necessary, but this does not necessarily enable us to express matters, negative and positive, pertaining to our work.

Many of the colleges also run lectures or meetings throughout the year for graduates. These are good opportunities to rub shoulders with practitioners of your discipline and to learn new techniques. We recommend that you attend them as they are very helpful. These do not have to be formal and expensive courses. Casual contact can also be reassuring to the newly qualified and experienced therapist alike. Seek out openings to meet other people. You may be surprised by the positive benefit of these occasions. Do not lose contact with

Make a note of the 1991 dates

The Health Show

4–7 July 1991 · OLYMPIA · LONDON

The Health Show at
London's prestigious Olympia 2
Exhibition Hall is the largest
public health and fitness show
in the U.K.

Special feature areas cover
natural therapies, healthy eating,
fitness, organic growing
and green living.

One entire floor is devoted to
natural therapies and includes a
demonstration stage and a
Practitioners Lounge.

Further details from the organisers,
Swan House Special Events Ltd

LONDON
TOURIST BOARD AND
CONVENTION BUREAU
MEMBER

Swan House Special Events Ltd.

Holly Road, Hampton Hill, Middlesex TW12 1PZ
Tel No. 081 783 0055   Fax No. 081 783 1678

Member
a|**e**|**o**
Association of
Exhibition Organisers

friends and colleagues from your college. Once you have graduated it is easy to say that you do not have the time or the means to attend annual reunions or conferences. They are important for your well-being. These contacts may also provide you with valuable business contacts, ideas and opportunities to expand your practice.

Beware of gurus

It seems that each profession has one or even several. They may appear to have a special charisma and knowledge and they do not only appear in spiritual or religious orders but in all walks of life. You can have financial gurus, literary gurus, medical gurus, political gurus and so on. Learn from them certainly, but do not enslave yourself to them. At whatever stage you are, you have to accept your position and be your own person. There are certain guidelines that need to be adhered to, concerning your own therapy, and your training will hopefully have covered those. With them in mind, there is a large area for individual flair and input to create your personal image.

Chapter 11

TROUBLESHOOTING

What can go wrong? Impractical overgenerosity. Mismanagement of capital. Tying up money in stock. PR checks: are you doing enough? High overheads. Scruffy premises. Problems with your receptionist and how to solve them. Housecalls.

There are many reasons why clinics and practitioners fail to be successful. The most obvious one is that the practitioner is not sufficiently skilled in his profession. We assume that our readers are skilled and competent and that they keep on expanding their knowledge, however experienced and learned they are. There are also very knowledgeable and effective therapists who are fundamentally exhausted by healing. They are unable, for a variety of reasons, to listen to problems and illness without becoming sapped of energy. In the chapter on 'Burn Out' we make suggestions to combat this problem of sensitivity.

A more concrete reason for a lack of success is charging too little for one's services. The practitioner's fees are too low and do not meet all the expenses. If this is true in your case ask yourself why you are charging too little. Do you feel unworthy of asking for more money? Refer to Chapters 1 and 7 and analyse why you are in this predicament. When you are prepared to charge more, phone around the area and find out what other therapists are charging. Find an average price which you know will adequately meet your bills and which you are comfortable charging. Remedy this immediately. It is silly to undervalue yourself and consequently go out of business. Also remember that you must review your fees annually to keep them in line with inflation.

You may prefer to establish a scale of fees with reductions for children and OAPs. This is a reasonable idea but has inherent failings. Many OAPs in affluent towns can well afford you. Many children take up much of your time and their parents are well off. Many working people struggle. Perhaps it is better to set your fees at a blanket rate and then have the flexibility to reduce them when you come across real hardship. We know a private doctor who worked in a rural area. Many of his patients were extremely affluent and well able to pay for his services. Some were not but were very good fishermen. They paid for their consultations in fresh salmon and trout. The doctor was happy and so were the fishermen.

Payment in kind is an interesting alternative if you can work it out to mutual advantage.

Impractical Overgenerosity

Another failing is overgenerosity. It is very British to be embarassed by money and want to give things away for free. You have managed to charge adequate fees for a consultation. On top of this you have prescribed remedies, supplements, Bach Flower Remedies, and herbal tablets which you supply. You are unable to ask for more money and include these in the price of the consultation fee. Your profit plummets and you have effectively given away half of your time for nothing. If you cannot charge for remedies do not supply them. Ask your patients to send away for them or buy them, if they can, from a health food shop. Do not be tempted to give them away. You will soon go out of business.

Another stumbling block is the mismanagement of capital. Are you tying up too much money in stock like remedies, vitamins, and minerals for too little return. It may seem sensible to order enough to last you a year but if you do not have enough to pay the bills and are paying interest rates on an overdraft this may be a big mistake. Review your stock situation and ask yourself how efficient and sensible the system is. Just how much money are you making? A service is only sensible if it is not breaking the giver.

You may find that you have too few patients coming to you. Ask yourself honestly if you are *expecting* patients but doing little to attract them? Reread Chapter 8 on publicity and write a check list of everything you can do.

You may also be able to join a register of practitioners for your area. Does your college hold one and recommend graduates? Are you a member? Find out if membership to appropriate societies brings this and other added bonuses and join. Also, let your colleagues in natural medicine know you are there and meet with them. They may refer patients to you or be willing to offer advice. You are not necessarily in competition with them and they may be too busy and want to refer patients to you. **You will not know until you find out.**

Look in the mirror and assess yourself honestly. Is your approach working? Is your attitude healthy? Do you really love your job or are you doing it for hidden reasons referred to in Chapter 14 about burn out? Give your personality an MOT. Are you relating to people well or are you being egotistical? Do you exude confidence or are you afraid of what you are doing? If you cannot assess yourself honestly because your nose is too close to the glass, take your courage in your hands and ask friends and colleagues for pointers to improve your working self. It is either that or fail.

If you lack confidence isolate your weak subjects and study more. This can take the form of home study and does not necessitate going on expensive courses. After all, you have the time if you are not busy. Meet with colleagues and talk over difficult cases. Couple study with a revamp of yourself. Use the confidence enhancing exercises you know each day or learn new ones. Do not accept second best. Add to these self-improvement exercises and set your goals. See success and create the future. **You can do it!**

The less tangible reasons for a lack of success are sometimes easier to tackle than practical reasons. Are your clinic overheads too high? Is your clinic located in an expensive high street when it could function just as well in a cheaper location? Can you share your rent with another practitioner? Alternatively, are you working in the sticks where no one can find you and there is no transport? In either case, you may have to cut your losses and pull out. Find a better location that is practical, affordable and that your patients can find. Be realistic about where you work. It is very important to set up clinics where people will come to you. We know of a very capable person who started a business unrelated to natural medicine. He had all the knowledge and experience to run his business but he sited his premises in a location that had potential but needed advertising. He did not do any effective marketing and waited for his customers to come in. As a manager he was very capable but as a promoter of his business he was a dismal failure. He did not have the financial resources to pay his rent until trade picked up (as it would have done in time) and he therefore had to close.

Do not throw good money after bad if you have made a mistake with your premises. Weigh up overheads with accessibilty and write a realistic business plan with cashflow and profit forecasts. Do not be naive and optimistic by paying high overheads or working in remote surroundings. You need a compromise between the High Street and the middle of nowhere.

Is your clinic off-putting to look at? It may look run down or plain scruffy from the outside. It may have an inadequate sign. It may be dark and dingy inside. Whatever appearance, you are probably only faced with a cosmetic problem that a lick of paint and a new sign would solve. You have the time so get painting and give that clinic a face-lift. Make it pleasant to visit. Fill it with plants and light colours. Put some positive thought and hard work in and patients will come.

We know of a therapist who had a good location on the high street in a market town near the main bus stops and railway station. He should have had no problems attracting custom. Unfortunately, the exterior of the clinic had not seen a coat of new paint in years and was a smoggy brown colour. The inside was not much better and reminded one of a postwar black and white film based in a deprived urban area. It was grim. Needless to say, he was not very successful. He did not need to spend huge sums of money. He just needed to inject a little energy and light. He did not and eventually had to leave.

The Most Important Person In The Clinic?

You may have a clinic which is reasonably priced, well located and pleasantly presented but with a receptionist who does not work in your interests. You can solve this easily by spending time with her. This person is a crucial ingredient to your success. She answers the phone to enquirers and books appointments. She is in the front line and the first person your new patients will meet. If she is not well informed or is offhand she will not attract the public. She will lose you custom and cost you a lot of money. Train your receptionist. Give her leaflets and books to read. Show an interest in her and give her time. Make sure she knows your subject well and can answer basic questions. Give her pointers in telephone techniques. If she is loyal to other practitioners in the clinic but is not you, ask yourself why. What can you do to change this? Are you paying enough? Do not treat the receptionist like an inferior. This is the best way to create an enemy. After all, why should you be superior because you are a practitioner? This professional snobbery is unfortunately not uncommon in medicine and is unwise.

Your receptionist simply may not be the right person for the job. You may have to replace her to survive. You have to consider this option. No one likes firing people but good management requires it sometimes.

Housecalls

Housecalls too are a tricky point. You must consider the time spent getting to the patient's home, the cost of petrol and the wear and tear on the car. If you take two hours to make a housecall you cannot charge for one hour. Try to arrange calls at the beginning or end of the day. If you dash out during the day, or even at lunchtime you lose more time.

Finally, what sort of patients are you attracting and why? Again, this goes back to image. If you walk the middle way and are not extreme in what you wear, or in your choice of location or the environment in which you work, you will attract a variety of different types. We are not suggesting that you become bland and boring, just that your personality is not so intrusive that it alienates the mainstream of people.

Chapter 12

DIFFICULT COLLEAGUES

Partnership agreements. Working with friends. Constructive plain speaking. Brainstorming. Mixing marriage and business. Colleagues with marital problems. Personality. Ambition. The 'special' therapist.

In your time as a therapist you will come across many difficulties with your patients and, unfortunately, with colleagues. This is one of life's laws. The human personality is complex and inevitably there are clashes and misunderstandings. This chapter is not a rogues gallery of what goes wrong in professional life – we do not have all the answers! But it is written to warn you of the pitfalls you may encounter. It is also written to offer you a practical way of avoiding some difficult situations.

We have mentioned before that it is essential to have a formal agreement with your partner(s). A gentleman's handshake is not enough. Be clear on every level: from who takes care of the maintenance of the clinic, to who pays the rent to the landlord and what percentage you gain from selling any remedies or supplements on behalf of the clinic. Do not leave business to unspoken goodwill. You will find yourself resenting situations that arise which threaten to poison your relationships.

Before you sign any agreements find out about your partners or associates. Are they trustworthy? What work have they done before? What is their business experience? Who will take responsibility for the books and the money? Can they give you good bank references? If they are personal friends, sit down and assess their personalities realistically. Are they excessively tidy and meticulous and will that trait irritate you if you are a happy-go-lucky type?

When you work with friends, a different aspect to their personality may emerge. Someone whom you thought was so laid back and relaxed may be really rather lazy and sloppy in business. That charming relaxed person is, in fact, a liability as a partner. Because he is a friend you may feel that you cannot speak plainly to him as this would endanger the friendship. Your resentment builds up until one day you bite his head off at something apparently inconsequential. A huge row develops and you are cast as unreasonable. Of course, there is a background history at work but time has eroded your reason. You see red!

Friendship requires negotiation as much as business partnership. If you do work with friends you must put aside the niceties of friendship and be open with each other. Do not be afraid to say that you don't like the way a colleague operates. Offer constructive alternatives when you criticise and be tactful, but speak your mind. Allow others to treat you in the same way. If you are open to suggestions and approachable in turn, it will make your opinions less threatening and it will diffuse many potentially volatile situations.

Brainstorming

The best business decisions are often made during 'brainstorming'. That is, when two or more people get together and throw out ideas. The more heated the session the better. We, your authors, have worked together on a number of projects. We do not always agree on business matters, having different approaches. One of us is impulsive, the other is reflective. Yet in other ways we share many characteristics. We are aware that tension can build up. If we allow ourselves to have a good session constructively arguing, disagreeing, throwing out ideas and not worrying about the impact on the other person, we actually manage to be creative. If we mind our 'p's and 'q's we achieve very little.

Intrinsic to brainstorming is trusting your colleagues. There is nothing like an animated difference of opinion in a meeting to get the adrenalin flowing and the ideas germinating. If you work with your friends there can be marvellous times but it is not all a bowl of cherries. Be sure you can argue and shout without resentment and confrontation as well as be supportive and pleasant. This will enable you to have a more dynamic and successful business relationship.

Mixing Marriage With Business

You may decide to form a partnership with your spouse. Marriage (or its equivalent domestic arrangement) and business are often mixed and can be a successful cocktail. There are obviously advantages to being attached to your partner on a personal as well as financial level. You are both working towards the same goal and all the successes and problems are shared. There will be little chance of both of you not being able to understand working problems if you share the same business. Any money you make is yours to share if you choose to and mutually enhances your life (although it can be taxed separately!). You are likely to get tremendous dedication from each other and to work very hard.

All these positive aspects presuppose that your relationship is healthy and you and your partner are not the kind that require a good deal of independence and space from each other. Whatever you do, do not start a business to heal a marriage. It is like having a child to grow closer. The added work load and responsibility are more likely to drive an immovable wedge between you. Like your friends, be sure that you can confront your partner in business with differences of opinion without having a huge row. The relationship cannot be the same as your personal one. You must have a completely separate persona which goes to work and deals with problems. Do not take resentments home with you. There is also an issue of competition. You may find that you are unconsciously competing with your spouse. Who is the busiest, the best, the most sought after practitioner, the most competent manager? Beware of the evils of comparison. Husbands and wives who work together have to be careful not to compete. Remember, you are not running against each other. You are running in a relay race in the same team.

The easiest trap to fall into is allowing your practice to take over your life together as a married couple. You even find yourself talking about work in the bath. (This is actually an excellent place to relax and talk over ideas and problems, we have found!) Beware of becoming so immersed in your business life that you lose touch with the person you fell in love with. Make rules. Go out together regularly and decree that you do not discuss business for that night. Make some part of your life sacred and do not let work trespass into it.

You may also find it a strain seeing a loved one 24 hours a day, 7 days a week. Your relationship becomes a hothouse with no room for you to stand back, breathe and create perspective. If you work and live with your partner, it is essential that you both have outlets which are separate. This may be a hobby or a friend who you go out with. It is also essential to create a space in your life when you are on your own. You cannot be two all the time. Spend time alone reflecting on your day/week/life. You may formally create a reflective meditation time or you may prefer to walk the dog alone. Whatever your style, do it. Don't scrimp on 'self' time. This is not selfish and inconsiderate to your partner. It recognises what you are, an individual who needs time alone to recharge batteries and get your own head in order. You will be more pleasant to live with as well.

Being closely linked in business and at home can cause undue stress on a relationship. It often brings about the end of both the partnership and the relationship. Before entering into such an arrangement think very deeply about the implications of working together. Combining a happy business and personal relationship is very difficult and requires hard work in both areas.

Marriage problems not only affect business between couples. You may find yourself in partnership with a therapist with a marriage on the blink. Once upon a time there was a very capable practitioner who had a very busy clinic and practised his discipline competently. Unfortunately, his marriage was in a terrible mess. This man was an impulsive, reckless character. He was highly intelligent, but flawed. His mind ran on so fast that he lost control of it when under stress. One day he did not appear at his clinic where he was in partnership with four other practitioners. His partners were naturally concerned and contacted his wife. He had disappeared. It unfolded that he had absconded with the clinic's quarterly rent for an impromptu holiday in the Mediterranean and did not return for a month, leaving colleagues, patients (not to mention wife and kids) in the lurch. An extreme example perhaps, but truth is always stranger than fiction.

Personality Differences

Practitioners can present other more subtle problems. Personality is always a bugbear. A 'new age' therapist with a more abstract, 'spiritual' approach may not necessarily get on with a practitioner who approaches his work in a more conventional, three piece suit mode! There is also the question of qualifications. A qualified medical doctor practising as an homeopath with a minimum of homeopathic training may feel that he or she is a better practitioner than a professional homeopath who spent four years at college part-time and cut his teeth on many years of seeing patients. The truth is that neither is probably any better than the other. Competence is reflected in the depth of understanding of the subject and in the commitment to private study.

Ambition

Another problem which you may encounter in a shared clinic is ambition. It is not unknown to have patients filched from under your nose by an over zealous receptionist working in the interests of one practitioner and not in the interests of the clinic. Beware of this when you rent space in a clinic managed by one practitioner. You can always get your friends to check by telephoning for appointments and discovering a definite bias to one therapist!

It is appropriate to mention again the importance of your receptionist. She is your representative and the first person your patient is likely to encounter when making enquiries about your practice. A receptionist sets the whole tone of the clinic. If she is intelligent, committed, helpful and kind your patients are more likley to feel welcomed and valued. If she is abrupt and uncaring, knowing little about natural medicine, you are unlikely to be running a successful practice. Finding the right staff is essential and training and nurturing them is of equal importance. Do not scrimp on your time and care when it comes to your receptionist.

Training is very important when it comes to confidentiality. Your receptionist will be filing patient's notes and overhearing conversations. Just as your professionalism depends on your ability to retain your patient's confidence by being the soul of discretion, your receptionist must also be able to maintain absolute confidentiality.

Another difficult aspect of ambition can occur in a clinic when a practitioner takes on a dubious new scheme to make money and uses the premises to promote his activities. This may involve a fabulous, expensive but unproven supplement course, elixir of life or even a therapeutic theory. Some of the slimming courses sold are of a dubious nature. Some of the 'get rich quick' pyramid selling methods also only benefit the few who sell to the many. Beware!

The 'Special' Therapist

A final note on the subject of problems with colleagues. Beware of the therapist who regards himself as special and sees his healing abilities as a sign of his spiritual development. This is an easy trap to fall into when one is in the profession of solving other people's problems. The ego has a tendency to run away with itself. The patients treated endow the therapist with a sense of power because they themselves *need* to believe that only an outside, supernatural force could possibly heal them. The regenerative forces of nature inherent in the person that are unlocked by the therapy then take second place to the 'channel', the guru who has performed the miracle. This kind of therapist mistakes his own egotism for spiritual development. He takes nature's glorious regenerative powers and sticks his own name tape on them. This is *not* honest. He steals hope by placing a personal monopoly on healing and sometimes may even use his abilities to manipulate and harm others.

Chapter 13

DIFFICULT PATIENTS

Palliative treatment. Steroids and strong medication. Repressed physical and emotional symptoms. The dangers of interfering with allopathic medication. Tranquilliser addiction: working with the patient's doctor. Abreactions. What not to treat when starting out. How to approach difficult treatments. Patients who ignore instruction and advice. Patient preferences. Men, women and sexual exploitation. False accusations. Transference, sexual or otherwise.

Natural therapies can help almost all symptoms and complaints on mental, emotional and physical levels of being. There are times, however, when you will come up against patients who, because of suppressive treatment in the past, will make it impossible to effect a cure. In such cases you may be palliative, which will allow the patient a certain level of well-being under the circumstances. Remember that you do not have to work miracles. Your job is to improve the patient's quality of life. There are instances when unfortunately a complete cure is not realistic.

The Palliation Approach

You may come up against cases where steroids have been used over many years. These would need the palliation approach. To attempt to take the patient off medication could be very dangerous and if you succeeded, the immune system would be so depleted you would not have much vitality to work with. Even if a cure was in sight, giving up steroids may cause a massive aggravation of the patient's symptoms (as in the case of steroid creams to suppress eczema). Will your patient be able to go through months of deep discomfort and disfigurement to effect a cure? It takes great faith and resolve on the part of the patient and practitioner. Is your patient ready to do it and can you provide the level of support needed? Only you can answer these questions. If either of you cannot, do not go through with it. Be realistic and assess each case on an in-depth and individual basis. Every situation has its own colours.

There are times when your treatment will unlock a multitude of suppressed or repressed physical or emotional symptoms. You may feel that you are unlocking

Pandora's box and countless negatives are escaping which are better off left undisturbed. Depending on your discipline, these may take the shape of emotional abreactions or physical, emotional or mental aggravations. Unless you handle these carefully they may frighten your patient and no therapeutic effects will occur. It is important that there are no misunderstandings and that the patient understands the process. The practitioner must be very supportive and confident that the treatment is reaching the root causes of disease and having a curative effect. Do not mistake these reactions for a simple degeneration as the disease takes its course. They are very different. Only good training and clinical experience can prepare you to distinguish between the two.

In some cases, it may be positively dangerous to interfere with allopathic medication. The side effects can be extreme. A patient with high blood pressure is an example. Changing his dose of medication may kill him. You can, however, treat this patient without touching his medication and relieve other symptoms, apart from high blood pressure. Ultimately, you are being palliative again. You are compromising holistically by only treating part of the person but you are relieving suffering whilst avoiding any disastrous reaction by leaving the allopathic medication well alone. Most practitioners are well aware of their limitations. It is always best to err on the side of caution.

The ideal of complementary medicine is to return the patient to a 'natural' homeostasis, to get the patient to a level of well-being in which the patient is free of all medication, even natural remedies. To become a slave to addictive medication, with side-effects, is like serving a prison sentence with no hope of ever becoming free.

Some drugs are necessary for certain conditions. For example, tranquillisers can be useful to help people overcome selected situations in their life like the loss of a loved one, divorce, or some other stressful experience. If the prescription is for a limited period this is fine, but there is a danger that the patient is left on tranquillisers for too long. Then when the patient wants to come off the drug they find it very difficult to do so. The withdrawal symptoms can be appalling and are well documented.

Working With The Patient's Doctor

Nevertheless you can work with the patient's doctor if he is cooperative. Write him a letter telling him that you are treating his patient. This is courtesy. Tell him that your patient has chosen to stop taking tranquillisers with the help of natural medicine. Any attempt to kick a drug addiction should be received well. Then you can decrease the dosage of the tranquillisers whilst substituting natural remedies to alleviate the anxiety and other more physical withdrawal symptoms.

This will obviously happen over a period of time depending on the individual. When the patient is finally off tranquillisers and just taking natural remedies, then because they are non-addictive and have no side effects you can stop the remedies. If handled correctly the transition can be a relatively painless one and you will have a happy and grateful patient.

We advise you to be very discriminating when you start in practice and indeed throughout your working life. Do not take on cases which are too much for you. This may be through a lack of experience or a lack of personal resources. Some people are tougher than others. If you are sensitive, work within your limitations. Do not overstretch and exhaust yourself. You will be no good to anyone.

Abreactions

Emotional abreactions need to be very carefully controlled. The patient has to feel that they are distanced from what they are seeing. It is very important that your training prepares you properly for these situations. If it has not, spend time studying the subject and speak with colleagues in the same field. The patient may also deal with these emotional revelations well at the time and then go away and feel ashamed, afraid, angry with you, or a mixture of these and/or other complex reactions. Prepare them. Talk it through. Be confident in yourself and do not be afraid of abreactions. They are therapeutic when managed properly.

You may also find yourself with a patient who reacts in an apparently negative way to treatment, whose symptoms are aggravated. He is physically much worse yet he 'feels better in himself', copes well and is more positive mentally. Despite increased discomfort, he is happy with the changes. The amelioration of physical symptoms may well follow. (This is dependent, of course, on the type of treatment you are offering and the nature of the complaint.)

Problems do occur when the patient is not prepared for the aggravation and misunderstands it, thinking he is worse off for the treatment. He blames you for making him worse. If you have not described the possibility of aggravation or lose confidence when it occurs, you will lose the patient and his trust in natural medicine. The key words here are *communication* and *confidence*. You must talk to your patients and believe in yourself. Then difficulties are less likely to arise.

Treating Serious Problems

We would not advise new practitioners to treat serious problems like long-term anorexia, psychosis, schizophrenia, chronic depression and patients with violent tendencies without a back-up system and support from experienced practitioners. We also mentioned high blood pressure. There are also other physical disorders which are life threatening and need informed handling. We are not saying they cannot be treated, we are just advising great caution. Know your limits and work within them.

An obvious example of this is cancer. Natural medicine can benefit cancer patients and need not always be merely palliative (although the importance of relieving the suffering of the terminally ill should not be understated). The psychological disciplines also have a great role to play in treatment and we would not wish to steer a newly qualified practitioner away from this work. Just be aware of the depth of suffering cancer brings and the violent reactions which can be uncovered.

We advise that the therapist who has patients with illnesses such as cancer has certain rules. Require that they come to you with a doctor's letter which accepts that they are seeking your treatment. It is no good if their GP is violently opposed to them seeking alternative or complementary forms of treatment. If the GP is not cooperative then the patient must change their doctor. Today, far more GPs are sympathetic to natural medicine and there is usually at least one in your area who will not be actively negative when their patient consults a natural practitioner. You will be pleasantly surprised to find support in these ranks. If the patient does not have a GP's support, there will always be tension and conflict between patient and GP and that, in itself, is counterproductive to your treatment.

Agree on a three month trial period of treatment. If there is no improvement you must review the situation together. Do not endlessly and hopelessly treat someone. It is a death sentence to them and is exhausting and discouraging for you. All it does is improve your bank balance. Then you really are a quack. This is not a way to succeed as a practitioner.

Remember also that certain therapies do much to alleviate the suffering caused by radiotherapy and chemotherapy. You may not offer remission from the disease but can help with the painful and distressing symptoms. The important ingredient in this approach is honesty. The patient must know that you are not hopeful of a cure but that the therapy will improve the quality of their life. This honest approach must be handled tactfully. Some patients never come to terms with the terminal nature of their illness. Others face the certainty of death more easily. We cannot adequately deal with this difficult and sensitive subject in this book. We strongly recommend that every healer study the subject of terminal care. A classic book about the way in which patients come to terms with their death is *On Death and Dying* by Elizabeth Kubler-Ross (Tavistock Publications). Whatever your discipline, this pioneering study written in 1969 is essential reading. It is an uplifting and fascinating account and gives great insight to the reader.

Another guide to the success of your treatment is to revise your initial tests every few visits to check on the patient's progress and tell them the results. Frequently signs and responses will change more rapidly than symptoms. It is important always to look for the signs and not the symptoms.

Patients Who Ignore Advice

You will also find difficult patients who do not follow instructions properly and then blame you for a lack of improvement. You may have given exercises, dietary changes, a programme of relaxation, remedies or some other form of treatment which is not adhered to. The patient then blames you because the treatment has not worked. Close questioning will help you to discover if this is the case. Additionally, there have been marked improvements but these are ignored because the client is seeking a magical answer and has unreal expectations. Beware of this at the onset and prepare the client to be more realistic. If idealism persists there is little you can do except to be patient, explain the course of treatment and stand by. There are often deeper reasons for idealism. These are not your fault. Do not let them rattle your confidence.

Of course, there are some human beings in the world who are never going to be happy however carefully you explain the course of treatment and however much support you give. They will find fault, criticise and be angry with you. Recognise these carpers and do not blame yourself. Some people sustain and entertain themselves by always being right and by belittling others. You cannot change them. Do not let their negative attitude affect you. Maintain confidence in the face of adversity and carry on. Let them go. Their road is the hardest to walk and it is a lonely one.

Each To His Own: Patients' Preferences

As a practitioner you must also realise that personality can be a stumbling block. Whoever and whatever you are, some patients will not get on with you, like you or warm to you. The rapport will not be there, however well trained you are in techniques to establish rapport. If you cannot establish a therapeutic relationship do not worry about it. Not everyone can be on the same wavelength. Not everyone can like you. If you feel that a personality clash will interfere with the process of healing, send them to a colleague with whom you think they will get on better.

By the same token, there are times when a patient may be more comfortable with a therapist of their own sex. The obvious gender preference often occurs with women wanting female gynaecologists, but there are other circumstances when this occurs. You cannot change this. Let it work to your advantage when you can and accept that you cannot be all things to all men and women!

You may also find that some patients want therapists to be older. Having both been unmarried practitioners in our twenties, we are aware that being young and relatively inexperienced in life can be a disadvantage with older patients. They seek authority and see youthfulness as synonomous with a lack of wisdom and knowledge. Fortunately, not all patients have that attitude or the young practitioner would be short of work. Also time has a way of solving this problem! To compensate, you will often see younger practitioners taking on older forms of dress and being more serious than their peers who work in less age conscious jobs. For your own sake, if you fall into this category, make sure you have a place in your life that is young. Youth fades and age comes all too quickly.

Men, Women and Sexual Exploitation

Women therapists need to be aware of sexual exploitation from men. Cases of women being physically threatened are not unknown. Be very careful that others are about when you treat a patient of the opposite sex. Also, men can have false accusations made against them. There was a case a number of years ago of a male hypnotherapist who was in court for improperly treating a female client. The case was dropped. Who was telling the truth? Did he approach her indecently or was she fabricating evidence? Only they know.

There can be a more subtle form of sexual harassment which is unsavoury and counterproductive. A patient of the opposite sex may construct an elaborate sexual fantasy in therapy and come to you for the pleasure of doing this and not for the reasons initially given. Beware of unhealthy situations and do not trap yourself in them. If you feel uneasy with a situation **do not ignore those feelings**. Change it. You do not have to dump the patient but you can make a colleague of the opposite sex sit in on the consultation and disrupt the mind game.

Incidents of transference are well documented from the time of Freud. The patient comes to you for treatment and transfers onto you the needs inherent in a relationship with a parent/lover/sibling/spouse/daughter/son/guru/teacher figure (to name a few!). You represent whatever they feel they need. This can be a deeply unconscious self-deception laced with the fear of discovery. You are no longer simply the therapist but are imbued with meaning in the client's mind. What you say may become completely misinterpreted as you, the therapist, are no longer speaking as a practitioner but as healer/lover/daughter etc. You may become an ideal figure and all the desires inherent in that longed for relationship are foisted upon you. You find you are expected to live up to them too. It is a complex situation.

There was once a lady psychotherapist who was treating a male patient in his forties who was going through a difficult and lonely time after his divorce. They happened to find themselves in the same restaurant one evening and the patient was anxious to join the therapist's group and socialise with her. The therapist was aware that the patient put her on an impossibly high pedestal and so she sought to climb down unceremoniously. She lit a cigarette and shattered the ideals of the patient who had always tried to see her as an ideal perfect human. The patient never saw the therapist again. Perhaps she was wrong to transgress in such an obvious manner but she knew that the therapy was over and the attachment was unhealthy, preventing the patient from getting on with his own life.

Every practitioner has ways of dealing with this problem. Some retain an impersonal barrier between themselves and patients and rarely contravene that protective distance. Others deliberately reveal their less than perfect selves from the onset and do not allow their patients to construct fantasies around the therapist's alleged perfection! How you deal with transference must be personal to you. However, be aware of it and understand it. See the warning signs and act. There is a great difference between a grateful and satisfied client and an emotionally dependent one. If you allow transference then you are playing a game which you too are emotionally dependent upon. Why do you want to be parent/lover/sibling/spouse/daughter/son/guru/teacher? In such an eventuality we counsel: 'physician heal thyself'.

This is by no means a comprehensive list of difficult patients. Variety being the spice of life, we could write a whole book on the complexities of human nature but we hope that these few examples will stimulate thought and a plan of action should any difficult circumstances arise whilst you are running your own practice.

Chapter 14

BURN OUT

How to avoid, deal with and recover from practitioner burn out. Long hours of listening to and dealing with physical, emotional and mental problems. Cut off points. Letting go. Workaholics. Responsibility weighs heavily. Hobbies. Patients' unreal expectations. Sabbaticals. Oversensitivity and how to deal with it. Hidden agendas and self scrutiny.

People of all demanding professions are at risk to 'burn out' before their time. Their work literally makes them sick. The more responsibility they feel, the more likely they are to exhaust themselves. If you work for yourself the likelihood of this happening is compounded. It is hard to turn work away and impossible to delegate many of the tasks you have to perform, particularly if you are a natural health therapist. In addition to the long hours of listening to your patients' physical, emotional and mental problems, you have to promote your practice and run the business side of being self employed. This is demanding for even the most competent and brightest person. It is no wonder then that practitioners who spend long hours of listening to and dealing with physical, emotional and mental problems have themselves been known to fall ill and suffer from stress. Some have even had to call it a day and work in another profession.

Holidays

Fortunately for all people working in difficult but rewarding jobs there are basic rules which will help to avoid burn out. Firstly, holidays are essential. It is unwise not to take time out to reflect and recharge one's batteries. We know of a young woman who started a business. She worked seven days a week for almost four years and never took a holiday, claiming that she could not leave the business. By the time she was twenty-five she was too ill to continue her work and on the verge of a breakdown. She was mentally and physically exhausted.

On the other hand, we know of a very successful homeopathic doctor who leaves his practice in the hands of a colleague and takes extended breaks abroad, travelling and visiting relatives. He comes back refreshed and enthusiastic, ready to pick up his work. He has a punishing schedule with a number of busy clinics but is able to handle the pressure because he looks forward to holidays long enough for him to unwind in.

Why don't we take holidays? What is there to be afraid of? Fears are so often irrational. Our patients won't die if we go away. We will not go out of business. We can always get a colleague to mind the clinic and take care of emergencies should they occur. The underlying problem is fooling ourselves that we are indispensable. We become addicted to our work and afraid to leave it. We inhabit a familiar world with safe routines and become trapped in them. Going away becomes threatening. The more stressed we become, the more difficult it is to leave and the more we need to. Do not hesitate. Take those holidays. They are an essential part of your survival plan!

Cut Off Points

Another trap of the self employed is not having a cut off point. There is no differential between work and home. Even if you do not work from home you take work home with you. This is compounded when the telephone is used for both private and business calls. Where can you escape to? Our answer is to install an answer phone and use it when you need to have some privacy at home. Have at least one day a week when you do not think about or discuss work, let alone do any. Have a time of the day which is private and nothing to do with work. Be strict about this. It pays dividends.

A practitioner we know used to work fourteen hours a day, six days a week. He found that he was no longer enjoying his work and was becoming highly stressed. He decided to cut his week to eleven hours a day, four days a week. The practitioner is now enjoying life, is in good health and is now more successful than he was working every available hour. It is no good being busy and affluent if you are unhappy, unwell and unable to enjoy the fruits of your labour.

Remember that orthodox medical practitioners are able to place the responsibility of cure on the drugs that they prescribe. The drug can be blamed if the treatment is unsuccessful thus deflecting the responsibility from the doctor. For many natural practitioners, there are not even any remedies or herbs to rely on. Even if remedies or medication of some sort are used, it is largely or solely the skill of the practitioner who tailors the treatment to the individual patient that successfully instigates cure or otherwise. The responsibility weighs heavily. Never underestimate the exhausting effects of practice and do not overstretch yourself.

Hobbies

Many practitioners have interesting hobbies which provide the necessary escape and recreation in their lives. We know of devoted windsurfers and surfers, mountaineers, bee keepers, fly fishers, yachtsmen and even rugby full backs.

THE EASIER WAY TO BOUNCING FITNESS FOR YOU AND YOUR PATIENTS

Enjoy effective exercising with just a few minutes on the PT Bouncer everyday

See what the PT BOUNCER can do for you:

* Improves lymphatic drainage
* Detoxifies the body
* Helps burn off excess fat
* Improves circulation
* Improves heart muscles
* Strengthens all body cells
* Lowers cholesterol levels
* Increases resistance to disease
* Improves oxygen supply
* Improves co-ordination
* Improves balance
* Helps relieve tension
* Tones up all your muscles
* Increases energy and vitality

PT Bouncers are being used today in the treatment of rheumatism, arthritis, sports injuries and cystic fibrosis. A safe and gentle form of exercising, the PT Bouncer is also used for physiotherapy and post natal toning.

Exercise on the PT Bouncer is easy and enjoyable for all the family. It is also ideal for the physically handicapped, the blind, the elderly and for gymnasts' and athlete's training.

For further free information, contact:

PT Leisure Limited
Apollo 4
Olympus Park
Bristol Road
Gloucester GL2 6NF
Tel: 0452 883588
Fax: 0452 883594

Whatever absorbs you and provides fun will do you good. It is far too easy to become too serious. You find you cannot unwind and let go of all the pain and suffering that you encounter in a working week. It becomes a part of you. Whatever kind of person you are, do not forget to enjoy life. Even healers should get a day of rest. Don't worry about what people think you should do as a healer. Stereotypes are thrust upon us all. Do what *you* want to do.

Another essential rule is for you to use the proven techniques that you recommend to your patients. Use relaxation and meditation techniques, take exercise and eat well. Do not become obsessive about bodily purity at the expense of mental release. It is no good being paranoid about junk food and alcohol to the point of never wanting to meet new people and go into unknown (and therefore uncontrollable) social situations. Stress is more damaging than the odd bacon sandwich. Moderation in all things is a sensible approach.

Patients' Unrealistic Expectations

Therapists are often placed on pedestals by their patients and cannot live up to these unreal expectations, i.e. they never get sick, they are always in control, they never have personal difficulties, they never get depressed, they are not beset by self doubt etc. It is normal for one person to look up to another. The danger is when the therapist starts believing in their patients' fantasies.

Another danger is when therapists push their own personal difficulties to one side. They are so 'other' orientated, busy solving everyone else's problems, that they neglect to deal with their own. These small crises build up and one day explode in their faces. It is impossible to function adequately with a volcano hidden below the surface, threatening to erupt at any moment.

Fortunately we are allowed to be imperfect, whatever some patients say. Everyone who works in the health field will tell you the shocked manner in which some people react when you get a cold. It is as if you are living proof that your therapy does not work! Do not be put off. It is a form of one-upmanship. Do not get involved in that game. You must learn to ignore and rise above such sarcastic comments.

Sabbaticals

Another option to avoid becoming drained is to take 'sabbaticals'. If you can afford to, this can take the conventional form of a period of study of your subject. You may have to take a job to support yourself and go back to practising at a later date. It is better to take that vital break in your life than to fall apart. You may not then have the choice of continuing.

Some practitioners prefer not to work full time. They combine a part time job with clinics. This is another way of diluting the impact of practising. The other job can be in a different field altogether or can be related. We have both run training courses and taught adult education courses in health studies. This is a good way of getting out of the clinic and meeting the public. Whether your other job is health related or not does not matter. As long as you are well, unstressed and enjoying life you are giving your clinics your best.

Sensitive Therapists

There are also therapists who are very sensitive people. They are tuned in to atmosphere and people's thoughts and feelings. They have long antennae and can often intuitively know what is going to happen next. This can help them in their work. It can also make them very vulnerable to their patients' negativity, disease and blacker emotions like anger, fear, desperation and hopelessness. If you are such a person you must protect yourself from this intuitive knowledge and develop techniques to make you more robust. Otherwise you will pick up on all the pain and suffering you encounter and live it out in yourself. Your practising days will be numbered as the strain will become too much.

There are practical steps you can take. Mentally build a wall or a cloak around yourself for protection. Visualise it in blue and recreate it before each consultation. See yourself being empathetic but remaining detached so that you are objective and therapeutically effective. After each consultation take off the cloak or climb over the wall and put aside all the patient's problems with a clean wind or bright, cleansing light. Wear certain clothes to work in and change after work. Do adopt a caring, healing persona but keep it specially for working time. Develop whatever protective system that works for you and use it. Do not underestimate the serious nature of being sensitive. If it is controlled it is a useful tool. Left uncontrolled, it can make you very ill.

Therapists like acupuncturists, chiropractors, reflexologists, and especially spiritual healers, who touch their patients in the process of treatment can be more vulnerable and aware of their patients' psychological and physical traumas. For those who do tend to experience this sensitivity, it is important to establish a ritual after each appointment. Practitioners wash their hands as a matter of course. Others also mentally centre themselves and remove the impression that the patient has left on them. Do whatever is effective for you personally but make sure you do it every time.

If you find these steps are only partially successful, your option then is to combine therapy with other work to minimise the strain. We have suggested that teaching and running workshops go well with practising but your other job could be quite unrelated. We know a very capable practice manager who combines her skills with working in a restaurant a few nights a week. She enjoys her more serious work at the clinic, with its therapists and patients and also the night life of the restaurant. She is able to do both jobs and enjoy them equally because they are in such great contrast to each other.

Hidden Agendas

Healing the sick is a laudable profession and is full of many truly kind and giving people. Great fulfilment is found in helping others. There is sometimes a hidden agenda behind this kind of work however, and every practitioner must look closely at their reasons for healing. This self scrutiny, from time to time, is not unhealthy, negative or cynical. It acts as a kind of protection against self delusion.

We all need to feel loved and important. Healing others can provide those feelings. It can also provide the comfort of having answers to problems and feeling in control intellectually. It is not unknown for healers to be captivated by the philosophy of their subject and to allow themselves to become a teacher or guru. This conveys the ultimate in a sense of well-being and control. We have alluded to this situation in Chapters 10 and 12. We do not think it healthy of anyone to set themselves up as an infallible fount of knowledge. All power corrupts and absolute power corrupts absolutely.

Being a therapist does give one status. It can act as a great therapy in itself for those who lack confidence. In giving to others we can also avoid the problem of being unable to give to ourselves. This is the martyr syndrome in which we sacrifice personal happiness for the happiness and health of others. It stems from Martha in the kitchen resenting the pleasure of those she serves. This is the danger of martyrdom. Resentment lurks in the background. A part of the martyr rebels against selflessness and wants to share in the pleasure. Practitioners who martyr themselves to their healing and give up personal fulfilment in the service of others forget a fundamental precept: you cannot give wholly to others if you do not give to yourself. Being 'self' aware is not selfish, it is survival and realistic. Martyrdom twists one inside and is a terrible drain on one's energies.

Another motivating factor in therapy is the need to unravel one's own mind. Some say that psychotherapists have the most introspective minds! They train to master their own problems and inadequacies and then pass that learning on to others. Added to this is the need to make sense of life by becoming a servant to others. If one gives, one takes on the mantle of being good and conquers the dark side of the self. This, when acknowledged consciously, is fine but we cannot be good all the time. Nature has two sides; light and dark, good and bad. We cannot inhabit one half of ourselves and repress the other half. It is a terrible strain living up to these exalted ideals. Many people have failed in their own eyes and felt profoundly guilty. If we are honest with ourselves and face both sides of ourselves, positive and negative, we have nothing to prove. Life is less of a struggle and more of a game.

Playing life as a game does not mean we have to be flippant. It is a question of remaining objective and remembering that we, as tiny individuals in an apparently vast universe, are only part of a mysterious cosmic process. Whatever your personal beliefs, if you hold on to the grandeur of the mystery you cannot take yourself too seriously. You can refuse to worry or take on all the world's problems. It is so easy to become drained by concern if you take responsibility for your patients' actions as well as your own. It is too easy to become exhausted and dissipated when you encounter the darker side of disease and psychic disturbance every day. Practitioners have to learn to let go and forget about the cares and pain of others. Again, this is not selfishness but survival so that you may 'live to fight another day'. A healer must be healthy to heal others.

Look closely at yourself. Ask yourself honestly what attracted you to your work. Accept those parts of yourself that seek respect, status, knowledge, control, the need to give to others, to understand oneself and the fulfilment of healing the sick. These are universal qualities. They present no danger when they are acknowledged. What is dangerous is not facing up to what motivates ourselves. That is when we walk a difficult way fraught with tension and self delusion. If we can be honest about our reasons for doing anything then we can accept the times when the reasons are not truly altruistic. Being partly selfish and flawed is human. It keeps our feet on the ground and eyes on heaven.

Chapter 15

WORKING ON THE FRINGES

The Law of Opposites and the Law of Similars. Orthodox diagnosis and its uses. Conditions for which you cannot legally claim cure. Conditions which must be reported to the local authority. Conditions to be wary of. Cooperation between disciplines, idealism and opening doors.

We often see alternative or natural medicine at odds with orthodox medicine. A homeopath will explain this in terms of philosophy and be very clear about the differing approaches of the two disciplines. Although other natural therapies do not follow the homeopathic philosophy to the letter, there are convergent points which illustrate how far apart so-called 'fringe' medicine is from the conventional approach.

The Law Of Similars and The Law Of Opposites

Homeopathy adheres to the Law of Similars and orthodox medicine adheres to the Law of Opposites. Both systems relieve symptoms but it is the way in which they are implemented that causes so much discussion and controversy. The Law of Similars or 'like cures like' introduces a substance or force which 'travels' in the same direction as the disease or illness, thus bringing about harmony in a gentle and permanent way with no side effects. The Law of Opposites works with a substance or force which 'travels' from the opposite direction in a confrontational manner.

An example of these differing approaches is the treatment of a patient with diarrhoea. The orthodox method would be to prescribe kaolin and morphine which causes constipation, morphine being a derivative of opium which paralyses the bowel. This action relieves the symptoms of diarrhoea but, because morphine also paralyses the tongue and brain, there are unwanted side effects.

The homeopath would see the symptoms as a reaction to an underlying cause. He would have faith in the body's reaction and not suppress the diarrhoea. Instead the treatment would seek to assist nature to expel the unwanted matter and to restore harmony as quickly as possible with a remedy that would stimulate the body's own regenerative healing force with no side effects.

To the orthodox doctor this approach is unscientific and potentially dangerous hogwash. He would argue that while the homeopath is working with apparently untraceable submolecular compounds the patient could die of dehydration. What is a paralysed tongue to the doctor in the face of a possible death? To the homeopath many allopathic drugs are dangerous and suppressive and merely mask symptoms which then reappear later in a more chronic and intractable manner. He knows his remedies work when prescribed on an individual basis for a particular patient with specific and individual symptoms. (A method of prescribing which cannot be tested by conventional clinical trials.)

The homeopathic philosophy of Similars dovetails in with many of the other natural healing philosophies. Acupuncture works on stimulating healing energies in the body. Hypnotherapy and Neurolinguistic Programming seek to unlock the healing power of the unconscious mind to restore harmony, both physically and mentally. Therapies such as herbalism and aromatherapy which use material substances of natural medicines work with the body and not against it.

Regardless of this fundamental difference of philosophy and practice there are occasions when the orthodox Law of Opposites is necessary and even lifesaving. You cannot set a fracture with a homeopathic remedy. There are other examples when the orthodox approach is preferable in the short-term, both from the point of view of relieving pain and anguish and for the individual patient's circumstances. We cannot turn our backs entirely on this approach. However, the Law of Similars or more natural approaches should be used in the first instance with most diseases to restore well-being, but with recourse to use more radical measures if necessary.

Orthodox Diagnosis and Its Uses

When a natural practitioner accepts this dual role of the two systems it is possible to work alongside allopaths. For example, conventional doctors are trained in diagnosis and often have a far wider knowledge of anatomy and physiology than many therapists. Their knowledge and experience can be invaluable. It would be remiss not to direct a patient with a lump under the arm to their GP for an opinion. Even if we do have experience of a complaint but consider that a diagnosis would benefit, we tell clients to visit their doctor. This is also a form of insurance for the practitioner. If the patient develops a serious illness, the practitioner has ensured that a conventional opinion has been sought and there can be no misunderstanding concerning diagnosis and treatment.

One hears horror stories from GPs with a bee in their bonnet about 'quackery'. A story regularly cited is of a patient suffering from headaches who goes to a natural therapist and the cause of which is diagnosed as 'stress'. Relaxation therapy and herbs are prescribed. Six months later the patient keels over with a terminal brain tumour. Exaggeration, you say? Using the GP for a diagnosis can do no harm and will protect you from any misunderstandings, let alone disasters.

Conditions For Which You Cannot Legally Claim Cure

Related to this subject is the Pharmacy Act. Natural practitioners are legally unable to claim that they can cure Brights Disease, cataracts, diabetes, epilepsy or fits, glaucoma, locomotor ataxia, paralysis or tuberculosis. It is actually forbidden by law for 'unqualified' medical practitioners to treat cancer and tuberculosis. Venereal disease can only be treated when there are no free facilities available.

Conditions Which Must Be Reported To The Local Authority

Conditions that must be reported to the local authority are: smallpox, cholera, diphtheria, membraneous croupe, erysipelas, relapsing, continued and puerperal fevers, malaria, tuberculosis, cerebrospinal meningitis and anterior poliomyelitis. There are also restrictions on attendance at childbirth. Because natural therapies treat the patient and not the symptoms, practitioners can avoid specific diagnosis and therefore not infringe on this act. Leave the specifics to the orthodox profession who are well trained in labelling disease.

Conditions To Be Wary Of

Besides the specific limitations already mentioned there are conditions to be wary of which warrant diagnosis. These include:

HEAD
Persistent headaches when it is unusual;
recurrent or chronic dizzy spells;
eye conditions and ear complaints;
chronic nasal obstructions;
swellings on the external neck or glands;

CHEST
a chronic or persistent cough, especially with spitting of blood;
wheezing due to a weak heart or a lung change;
pains through the chest (more often heart trouble than a lung condition);

heart palpitation;
shortness of breath on mild exertion;
waking up due to breathing difficulties in the night;

ABDOMEN
any swelling of the abdomen which occurs in a short time;
any painful areas above or below the navel, especially with indigestion;
pains on the right iliac area;
any localised mass with or without swellings or distention;
any abdominal complaint in pregnant women, especially if localised;
radiating pains to the groin, suggesting the involvement of the kidneys;
any changes in the bowel habit, especially for those over 50;
narrow or painful stools with dull ache in rectal area;
any bleeding whatsoever from the rectum;
black or bloody stools;

URINARY ORGANS
excessive frequency in urination;
large amounts of thirst and large appetite;
frequency of urination at night (not usually significant in elderly men);

GENERAL SYMPTOMS AND STATES
excessive weakness at any age;
any lump or enlarged gland anywhere, especially in the breast, armpit, groin, and neck;
continuous loss of weight even though eating well;
backache if severe and continued;
change of voice with painless lump in throat:
redcurrant or raspberry sputum;
vomiting without nausea and a change in character (brain tumour).

These conditions should alert you to the possibility of a serious disorder. Rather than terrifying a patient by inaccurate diagnosis, refer him to his GP. Let them call in the specialists. You can still treat the individual at the same time.

We recently had an example of treating a man with chronic pain in the lower back. He visited his GP for a diagnosis and was duly sent for an x-ray which revealed kidney stones. After visiting a specialist, a second x-ray was scheduled to enable him to decide whether to operate and surgically remove the stones. During this episode the patient received homeopathic treatment and made a change in his diet, drinking only mineral water, eating less animal fats and eating more vegetables. When the second x-ray results came through to the patient's delight and the consultant's perplexity the stones had disappeared yet the patient had not even experienced passing them in his urine (a painful experience).

The patient was happy to have had the security of an orthodox opinion, although delighted to have avoided orthodox treatment. The homeopath was happy to have assisted his patient's return to health. The GP made no comment and had no explanation for the disappearing stones.

Cooperation Between Disciplines

Another example of cooperation between disciplines is childbirth. A woman recently had a baby in a large general hospital. She practised yoga all the way through her pregnancy and went on walks, ate a sensible diet, attended National Childbirth Trust classes, read the right natural childbirth books and regularly saw a homeopath who prescribed remedies for general health and the birth. Despite all these precautions the birth was long, painful and she was unable to deliver without analgesia and assistance from the registrar. Without orthodox medicine the labour and birth would have been Victorian in its difficulties and pain and the baby would have died. Needless to say, baby and mother recovered quickly and are now fighting fit. The natural approach to childbirth would have been a disaster in this instance, but it is fair to add that short-term orthodox intervention in a situation that usually occurs once or twice in a woman's life has consequences which are rarely suppressive or serious.

Other examples of working together are when a patient wishes to conquer addictive drugs like tranquillisers. The practitioner and GP can arrange to cut down the doses gradually whilst the natural medicine relieves many of the withdrawal symptoms and the anxiety.

Similarly, patients with blood pressure can use natural medicine to help with the headaches but continue to take the drugs which treat the blood pressure. The therapist would be very unwise to take the patient off the orthodox drugs unless they had extensive clinical experience themselves in this field.

With cancer, hypnotherapists have worked with patients on visualisation techniques to shrink tumours, control pain and minimise the effects of radiotherapy and chemotherapy, not to mention the benefits of counselling, whilst the patient uses all the conventional methods of treatment. Homeopathy too can alleviate the suffering caused by the side effects of chemotherapy and radiotherapy. One system does not cancel out the other.

Orthodox medicine has its place in situations that are life-threatening like a burst appendix, or when a patient's quality of life is so low that alleviating suffering comes before anything else, or when the natural therapies have failed to work for various reasons (as when a patient has a history of suppressive drug use). We do not advocate indiscriminate use of orthodox medicine but we cannot close our eyes to it. How many patients do we treat who have never taken allopathic drugs in their life and are consequently free from their suppressive effect? Very few, which forces us to acknowledge its role in our patients' lives, for better or worse.

We, as therapists, cannot afford to build walls around our work and keep out conventional medicine. We should not be so idealistic that we are unable to see the benefits of working together. Certainly, doctors are beginning to accept natural medicine and give it a place in the healing arts. Not all of them are prejudiced. As research into natural medicine continues, 'science' will prove resoundingly the positive curative effects of the natural alternatives and the great arguments between the two sides will be silenced. We hope that before the multitude of chemicalised drugs and vaccines are administered to the patient, the natural therapies will be tried and gentler more holistic methods will be given first place in health care. We know that great changes will have to come before that utopian vision becomes reality, but no one can deny the welcome changes in the general public's attitude to natural therapies which have developed in the last thirty years.

Chapter 16

PREPARING FOR THE FUTURE

Property insurance. Accidental loss or damage cover. Unlimited indemnity. Public liability. Professional indemnity. Personal pension plans. Advantages of personal pension plans.

Having considered difficult patients and colleagues we now look at insurance and pensions for practitioners to protect us from unforeseen disasters! Insurance is an essential factor in any business. An unexpected loss can cause financial hardship and destroy many years of hard work. Nowadays you will be able to locate insurance companies that specialise in clinic and surgery cover at reasonable costs. With this in mind, you can arrange for an insurance policy designed specifically for your clinic to protect you from most of the risks your business might encounter. Standard cover will usually include the contents of clinic to a maximum of £100,000.

Property Insurance

Property insurance will cover you for specific perils like fire, lightning, wind damage, explosion, earthquake, aircraft, riots, civil commotion and theft. In the light of our unpredictable weather, this may be essential. Losing an uninsured roof would be a great misfortune.

Accidental Loss Or Damage Cover

You may decide to include accidental loss or damage which would cover incidents of dropping expensive equipment by anyone in the clinic. You could also cover yourself for damage outside the clinic. Say, for instance, you visited a patient's home and accidentally knocked over a priceless Ming vase. This would be unfortunate in itself but it would be far worse if your patient decided to claim compensation and you had neglected to cover yourself.

Insurance should also cover you for the loss of money in notes, coins and cheques on or off the premises for specific amounts. We know of a number of instances when busy practitioners have been engaged in consultation, the clinic's bell has gone, the receptionist has gone out to run an errand, and the cash box has been opened and the contents stolen. A tragic loss to a struggling new clinic can be avoided through careful insuring although be prepared to write off the first £50 to £100 in 'excess', a figure which you will have agreed to when acquiring the policy.

Burglary is a crime which is becoming increasingly common. We also know of clinics being broken into at night, windows being smashed and office furniture being damaged. Money has been stolen as well. Insurance will not take away the inconvenience but it will cover the financial loss. In Chapter 2 we give some thought to securing premises and valuables. We advise that you look at your property objectively and do what you can to protect it. Efforts to dissuade the burglar save time and heartache in the long run.

Unlimited Indemnity

Your insurance should also cover liability to employees with an unlimited indemnity. If your receptionist falls over your brief case and tumbles down the stairs, causing severe damage to her back, you will be insured for any claim against you. The employee will also be able to make a claim against the policy which will provide financial assistance during the time of treatment when she is unable to work. Few accidents are fortuitous but at least the employee will be protected against financial hardship and you will not lose sleep over the possibility of expensive legal action.

Public Liability

Practitioners should also cover themselves for liability to the public. This will insure you for up to £1,000,000 indemnity on any one occurrence. A patient may trip over your carpet or fall down the stairs and land on top of the receptionist! He may be struck on the head by a tile falling from your roof as he leaves the premises. Whatever the catastrophe, public liability is a must. It will enable you to sleep peacefully at night, secure in the knowledge that no one can bankrupt you by virtue of an unfortunate and unforeseeable accident. This cover should not, of course, allow you to neglect your premises and leave potentially hazardous items lying around the place. You do have a responsibilty to the public and your staff to make your clinics safe and secure.

Professional Indemnity

Professional indemnity is also essential for the practitioner to cover any charges of negligence or malpractice. This form of insurance is not so readily available,

ESTABLISHED 1933

PUBLIC LIABILITY/MALPRACTICE INSURANCE
Arranged by
HERRIOT INSURANCES LIMITED

**Bridge House, 27 Bridge Street,
Leatherhead, Surrey KT22 8HE
Tel: 0372 378804
Fax: 0372 372430**

Members of the British Insurance and Investment Brokers' Association

**We have been arranging all classes of
Insurance for Practitioners for over 50 years
and we welcome your enquiries.**

**The Malpractice Scheme is available on an
Individual or Group basis and cover can also
be obtained for Student Practitioners.**

although some insurance brokers will provide the service. The usual procedure when dealing with a broker is to send in your CV with details of your training, qualifications and experience. You must also state any known or reported claims.

Your college should offer you the opportunity to join a society of practitioners on graduation. This society usually negotiates a collective insurance scheme for its fully qualified members. The advantage of belonging to a society which provides this service is that they are able to negotiate a more competitive rate for negligence indemnity than an individual practising on his own.

Personal Pension Plans

After you have covered any disastrous eventuality on the property or negligence front, you may wish to consider personal pensions, an insurance policy for the end of your working life. When we are in our twenties and starting our careers we think little of four decades time and retirement. We wonder if we will live that long or if the planet will survive anyway. As the years creep up on us, we become aware that we have to provide for the future and that we may have missed valuable opportunities that make retiring less traumatic and more a time of achieving those things that we have never had the time to do whilst earning a crust. We vaguely think that our National Insurance contributions will provide for that time as well as for misfortune and unemployment. 'The State will provide.' Today, we no longer have the luxury of relying on state benefits, especially if we are self employed. Our National Insurance contributions do not automatically cover maternity allowance, sickness benefit, unemployment benefit or a pension which is not means tested.

The basic state pension provides a flat-rate income to keep the wolf from the door but it will only cater for the barest essentials in retirement and no more. It would be very hard to survive on it alone. Every penny has to be accounted for and any major expense and times like Christmas make severe inroads into any savings the pensioner may have. Because so many more people (especially women) are living beyond their sixties, retirement has become an important stage of life. It is therefore sound advice to make additional private arrangements. Having a personal pension in addition to a state pension eases the strain of these non-earning years which should be pleasurable, relaxed times. For the lucky few who have been in a position to plan ahead, the state pension is the jam on the bread. For many though it is a small pittance in a rather grim financial reality.

A good pension scheme could provide a regular income and a tax-free cash sum. A pension plan enables you to save money regularly during your working life to provide a reasonable income during retirement. If you have been self employed, and most practitioners will fall into this category, you could, on retirement, see your income drop by more than two-thirds by relying on the state scheme. It is an unfortunate fact that fewer than a third of the people retiring at sixty-five are financially independent.

The Advantages Of A Personal Pension Plan

Some advantages of a pension plan include:

a) Tax Savings on Contributions – this means your tax bill is reduced by £25 for every £100 you contribute, if you pay tax at the basic rate. If your tax rate is higher than basic rate your savings will be greater.

b) Tax-Free Investments – there is no United Kingdom income or capital gains tax to pay on investment profits.

c) Tax-Free Cash Sum – at retirement you can get 25% to 30% of benefits in a tax-free cash sum in addition to a pension.

d) Tax-Free Death Benefits – a lump sum should you die before age 75. Not subject to inheritance tax if paid to a designated beneficiary or a surviving spouse.

e) Repaying Loans Tax Efficiently – you can borrow an amount equal to the value of your fund on the security of other suitable assets, and the loan need not be repaid until the benefits are drawn.

Pension schemes vary from company to company, so before you decide, approach several companies to find one that suits your individual requirements. You may have an independent financial adviser. He or she can possibly demystify pensions for you and point you in the direction of a scheme which suits your particular requirements. Before you agree to any pension scheme, research this field very carefully and be sure that you have bought into a scheme which will suit you. Your circumstances may change over the course of your life and it is important to know that your pension scheme is flexible and able to reflect those changes.

It is also important to start a pension plan as early in your career as possible. Premiums are greater and returns are less substantial the longer you leave it. Without wishing to sound like an advertisement for the companies, it is wise to invest now rather than when you start to feel you need to!

Chapter 17

THE SINGLE EUROPEAN MARKET

Common Law and the Napoleonic Code. The Treaty of Rome. Exceptions to the rule and the Treaty of Paris. Vested interests of drug companies. Restrictions on herbs, homeopathic remedies, supplements and tonics etc. The importance of joining societies and organisations. Lobbying MPs and MEPs. Staying informed.

You would be quite justified in asking what the single European market has to do with becoming a successful natural health practitioner. The unpalatable reality is that the whole future of natural medicine is threatened by our entry into the Economic Community's marketplace. The relevance of '1992' is of paramount importance.

The old adage that we rarely appreciate something until we have lost it may well apply all too tragically to our freedom under British law to practise the natural therapies and buy over-the-counter health products. Similarly, few British people appreciate their ancient system of law until they fall prey to legal difficulties in foreign countries with less sympathetic procedures. They then realise the relatively 'liberal' nature of the British legal system and why it has been regarded as a philosophical benchmark for a set of rights for the common man (although theory and practice can be worlds apart).

Common Law and The Napoleonic Code

In Britain our Common Law enables us to do anything that is not specifically forbidden. In other European countries which operate under the Napoleonic Code, citizens can only do what the law expressly allows. In a general sense, Common Law has allowed for individuality and the great British cult of eccentricity. The Napoleonic Code, by comparison, stifles true genius by its repressive and uniform nature. How can you innovate when everything new and unaccounted for is regarded as in breach of the law?

Now we, your authors, are not British bulldogs who aggressively attack all aspects of a pan-European initiative and wish to hold on to our sovereign rights in all areas. We accept that blinkered patriotism has led to lost opportunities and horrific wars in the past. However, the implications of a single European market which requires, under the Treaty of Rome, that any law agreed in the Community must be enforced in every member country does not bode well for natural medicine. It means that where there is a conflict between the law of a member country and a law of the Community, the law of the country must come into line with the Community.

There are exceptions to the rule. If Community law seriously affects the people of a member country, arrangements can be made to release that country from those laws. The Treaty of Paris, for example, regulates and protects the steel industry in France and Germany. Each case is decided on its own merits.

How does this affect natural practitioners in Britain? All alternative/complementary practitioners qualifying from the various colleges in the UK have to date been able to practise with relative freedom under common law. Anyone can practice chiropractic, osteopathy, homeopathy, herbalism, manipulation, acupuncture, radionics, polarity therapy, hypnotherapy, aromatherapy, colour healing, psychotherapy and all the many other forms of healing. There are restrictions on claiming cure for certain diseases, treating venereal disease and attending women in childbirth as we elucidated in Chapter 15 but basically, we are free to carry out this work as we see fit. In other Community countries, only medically qualified doctors can practise the healing arts.

For example, a medical herbalist student trains for four years in college. We could argue that because the course is very rarely even partially funded by a local authority, this indicates the deep commitment of that student who balances study with a job or savings to finance the course. Remember that in America it is relatively common to 'work your way through college' and is not considered a stigma, far from it. An orthodox doctor trains for five years in medical school in subjects like drug therapy and surgery which are often unrelated to natural medicine and are a philosophical anathema to it. Yet on graduation, he can call himself an acupuncturist or homeopathic doctor without further training, or at very best, a short course. We are not implying that medically trained natural therapists are incompetent or worse than professional therapists. Far from it. We are merely pointing out that the bias is always with the established orthodox field which has sought to control medicine since its inception.

Few doctors are inclined to study natural medicine after years of orthodox training. It is too speculative in our current intellectual climate for the mainstream of medical practitioners and is not accepted by the main teaching hospitals. One day, natural therapies may be accepted by the orthodox professions, although we can expect that the multi-million pound drug industry will do its best to quash a liberalisation of medical practice. In the United States, homeopathy was adopted by the medical profession for general use at the beginning of this century but its popularity has declined (largely due to controversy stimulated by vested interests concerning its efficacy). Now it is difficult for patients to find the homeopathic treatment they want in most States. This could well happen in the UK if we adopt the repressive Community legislation and stifle consumer freedom to visit lay practitioners of our choice.

Of course, we accept that orthodox medicine has a well established place in our society. We are not so idealistic to suppose that all people should seek or indeed want the natural alternatives. What concerns us is an orthodox monopoly which will restrict or even stop talented, knowledgeable and well trained healers from practising their skills.

Restrictions On Natural Products

In addition to the Community laws concerning medical qualifications, there is a more worrying aspect which directly affects the consumer's right to purchase natural products over the counter. In Britain, we sell many supplements, homeopathic remedies, Bach Flower Remedies, tissue salts and tonics as foods which can be purchased from health food shops. In other Community countries these same products are only available in pharmacies and many of them are restricted and some are banned.

The tradition and practice of herbalism goes back many centuries. Until recently, we could buy most of the herbs commonly used without the supplier needing a licence or proof of the herb's lack of toxicity. Today, 2,500 herbs have already lost their 'licences of right' and up to another 1000 are threatened. Additionally, companies supplying herbs now require three times as much money to acquire those licences as they did five years ago.

Occasionally, we read alarmist stories in the press about 'toxic' herbs causing cancer and other diseases. Of course, if you feed large quantities of comfrey to rats and nothing else it is likely that the rats will develop a severe illness and die. What happens when you feed large quantities of paracetomol or aspirins to rats? They die a lot quicker than they did from their monomanic diet of comfrey! We wonder who perpetrates these scares and why?

We are not saying that natural medicines are not harmful in large doses or that they should not be treated with respect. Nor are we saying that natural therapists should be allowed to practise without adequate training and be subject to restrictions and discipline from professional bodies. What we are saying is that this matter is too important to ignore or leave up to our Government to defend. They say that the issue is not worth the time or money even though they are prepared to bicker over the wording on cigarette packets.

Affiliation To Accredited Colleges, Societies and Professional Bodies

If we thought that the single European market was the death knell for natural medicine we would not have written this book. What we do see as vital however, is that practitioners must become affiliated to accredited colleges, societies and professional bodies. Ideally, we should also create and support a single democratically constituted representative body as an officially recognised independent professional association to act for *all* the therapies. The reality of the current situation, given the enormous spectrum of natural medicine, is that some disciplines are more generally accepted by orthodox medicine and are thus less threatened by 1992. The more 'complementary' therapies are consequently less willing to join with the more 'alternative' therapies to fight for all branches of natural medicine as a whole.

We cannot fight these repressive changes and protect all the branches of natural medicine if we are not united. It is pointless and self destructive to bicker amongst ourselves as to which therapy or organisation is acceptable or superior. We must lay down standards in training and practise for all the forms of healing and join together to lobby Brussels to protect practitioners and patients alike. It will be a tragedy if some take the attitude, 'I'm alright at the moment, Jack!', whilst the practice of natural medicine by non medically trained practitioners is eroded and then finally outlawed in 1992 due to a lack of foresight and no united voice to speak for all the various disciplines.

Whatever kind of organisations emerge, they must be efficient and organised. We recently contacted an organisation for details of their activities and never received any information or even a reply. How can practitioners be expected to support a professional organisation if the organisation itself is haphazard and sloppy? We were very disappointed to encounter this sort of unprofessionalism and hope that this was an isolated incident. There is no reason for natural medicine organisations to be an outdated and inefficient. Why shouldn't they get their houses in order and create a united front? If that is what we really want (and we feel that without one voice our future is blighted), we must establish such an association. However, that one voice has to be efficient, professional and ready to enter the 21st century.

We are aware that the Government now believes 'very firmly' that it must be for each group to determine its own future development and has clearly stated this during a debate in the House of Lords on 9 May 1990. There are implications behind this statement which do not bode well for some of the natural therapies which are considered to be more 'fringe' or 'alternative' than so-called 'complementary' medicine. What concerns us is that whilst the more acceptable professions will be able to set agreed standards of education, accreditation and

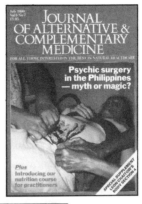

codes of practice, other therapies may be left out in the cold and the practice of them by lay or 'professional' practitioners outlawed after 1992. We are not suggesting that standards should not be set. Far from it. We just want to see all the therapies being treated fairly with an equal voice. Natural medicine contributes to the rich tapestry of our lives in this country. It would be very sad to see it curtailed.

As individual therapists we do have a duty to stay informed. We can subscribe to those publications and journals which report on the latest Community policy and its effect on natural medicine. We can stay in touch with our colleges and join our relevant societies. We can personally lobby our local MP and MEP. We can also inform our patients or clients of the current and potential political changes which deeply affect their right to seek relief from natural therapies and buy the herbs, supplements, remedies and tonics over-the-counter. Above all, we must call for and support organisations to lobby Brussels. Only grassroot pressure in Britain will effect compromise and cooperation on a national level for all the branches of natural medicine. Only a united voice will affect changes on an international level and protect our right to heal.

Chapter 18

THE REWARDS

The value of natural medicine. Success is not always measured in money. The rewards of healing and helping others. Becoming part of humanity. Health and Gaia: the integration of people and planet. The personal support system. Philosophy of success. Pragmatism. Thinking big. Personal fulfilment and freedom for philanthropy. Moving into the future.

The practice of natural medicine can be a uniquely satisfying profession. Patients come with apparently insoluble problems and are set on the road to health by the healing powers tapped by the various disciplines. Each practitioner has the privilege of watching nature at work, stimulated by established techniques or remedies. The essential simplicity of the systems used belies the mystery of how they work. Homeopaths talk of the vital force, hypnotherapists call on the infinite abilities of the unconscious mind, acupuncturists call it Chi or Ki. Whatever the discipline and its methods, there is an underlying thread which passes through them all, linking every practitioner to the invisible but potent regenerative force which heals and restores harmony.

There are always hidden rewards for the natural practitioner. This is not quantified in the gratitude of patients or the size of the bank balance at the end of the week. It is fascinating to study the healing process at work and the way in which the practitioner is merely an agent or instigator of the process rather than the director. We cannot 'claim cure' at all. A deeper process is at work. The patient heals himself and we watch. Often we find that our greatest 'successes' are when the patient hardly gives credit to the therapist. They feel better so quickly that they assume that confronting the illness and seeking help was curative in itself. A positive attitude has put the therapeutic power of the remedy or technique into second place in the patient's mind. The healing has been invisible. At such times we are aware that we are delving into a world in which we have little understanding. We know our methods very well. They are certainly not hit and miss. It is the process as a whole that is so totally unknown. Who can plumb the depths of the human 'bodymind'? Life lived on this level can never be banal or predictable.

It is also a privilege to enter the private world of so many individuals. We do not hand out prescriptions to queues of waiting sick. We have the time to get to know our patients and enter their worlds. How many harassed GPs would envy that time available? The days of the good old family doctor are long gone. Entering so many private realities leads us to appreciate that people, far from being alien and different, are touchingly similar. We share fears, pain, grief, joys, aspirations. Common denominators abound. The differences are shallow. Being a witness to the vast areas of common ground brings one in from the cold. We cannot be alienated outsiders. We realise that we do indeed share those human frailties. We become a part of humanity in a conscious and practical manner.

Beyond a sense of unity with individuals is the sense of unity with our world as a whole. The living, breathing force of Gaia, our Earth, becomes obvious. Our remedies and curative techniques are a part of this entire planetary system. Natural medicine cannot be divorced from Nature. The therapies tap into and are examples or touchstones of a larger regulatory process. Our planet is a self-regulating organism which continuously seeks homeostasis. The fabric of that system is a web of interdependent species which is our biological, ecological and, for some, our spiritual base. Natural medicine sees health in a holistic manner as integration of body, mind and spirit. It does not plunder resources but recognises nature's ability to regenerate and uses those forces with respect. It is only one logical step away to see personal and planetary health as indivisible. How can human beings be healthy on a sick and polluted planet? The equation is impossible. The very nature of our medicine is 'green'.

Living life by this integrated 'planetary' vision is a tall order. It is not always possible to carry out the ideals implicit in the philosophy. We may carry a torch for personal health and happiness but, by the mere fact that we inhabit a First World late twentieth century country, our lifestyle and what we consume are inevitably polluting and detract from the overall health of our planet. All we can do is minimise the damage and find realistic solutions to change the way in which we live.

The nature of our profession offers us the chance to meet and communicate with like-minded people and to create our own personal support systems. We are not trapped in a conventional and stultifying job with colleagues who do not share any of the same ideas as ourselves. There is a great freedom in marrying one's profession with one's personal philosophy. The Buddhists call this 'right livelihood', an essential ingredient in the right way to live.

These considerations form a very powerful base from which to work. In helping and healing people we give but we also receive. There is a great satisfaction in watching people return to health. We therefore owe it to ourselves to be accomplished at what we do in the healing sphere and to offer our services in the most professional and business-like manner possible. We need not be obsessed by business but merely equally skilled in the managing of our work as in the practice of our therapies. A sound financial base offers us the opportunity to get on with the real work of healing and to maintain health and well-being in ourselves. If we work from a practical, realistic but positive viewpoint, it is hard to fail.

Financial well-being is not the only end but it does convey freedom. If we are free from monetary worries we have the capacity to work with less distractions. The same applies to emotional and physical well-being. How hard it is to heal others when we are sick ourselves! Beyond a basic form of efficiency is the freedom to practise philanthropy and to 'give back'. Only a level of financial well-being allows that luxury. We all have our dreams. You may dream of free natural medicine clinics or courses in preventative medicine. You may have other philanthropic dreams which are nothing to do with your work but are still equally valid. In our own small way we may earn the freedom to practise an aspect of philanthropy. Success is not all taking. It can incorporate giving back as well.

Our future in terms of the planet as a whole always appears uncertain. This seems even more pertinent today. We cannot even be sure of the coastlines or weather patterns in the twenty-first century, let alone the shape of the single European Market. Yet we cannot be paralysed by what are, to the ordinary individual, imponderables. What we have to be sure of is our own direction and our ability to carry through our goals. If we seek personal excellence, or at least attempt our best, we are not just hiding our heads in the sand and ignoring the complex workings of the world we live in, we are fulfilling our own personal potential and benefiting others along the way. This is not a 'me' orientated map of the world but the philosophy of 'we' and 'us'. Our effects can stretch as far as we are able to spread them. The more professional we are, the more powerful our voices.

This book has been written to explore another dimension of the natural practitioner's profession. So much is written about the various disciplines, philosophies and their therapeutic possibilities. So little is said of the day to day running of a clinic as a small business. We hope that this book redresses the balance a little and enables the therapist to concentrate on the art of healing, whilst the mechanism of business runs smoothly and invisibly in the background.

Appendix

PARTNERSHIP AGREEMENT: AN EXAMPLE

AGREEMENT AND DECLARATION OF TRUST
between Practitioners A, B and C

This Agreement and DECLARATION of TRUST is made the First day of August 1990 between Practitioner A of the first part Practitioner B of the second part and Practitioner C of the third part all of which are hereinafter together called 'the Parties'

WHEREAS

1) By a Lease dated the 1st day of August 1990 and made between ANESTATE DEVELOPMENT LIMITED of the first part XPROPERTY MANAGEMENT LIMITED of the second part and the Parties of the third part the property situate and presently known as Unit 1 A Business Centre Health Road Newtown (hereinafter called 'the property') was demised to the parties for the term of one hundred and twenty five years from the 1st day of January 1988 at an annual rent of a peppercorn (hereinafter referred to as 'the Lease')

2) Planning approval has been granted by the Newtown District Council for use of the property as medical consulting rooms and the parties hereto have agreed to use the said property for these purposes on the terms and in the manner hereinafter appearing

3) The parties hereto have contributed to the purchase price of the lease of the said property in unequal shares and it has been agreed that the joint tenancy deemed to have been created by the said lease shall be severed so that the parties shall hold the said property on trust for themselves as beneficial tenants in common on the terms and in the shares hereinafter set out

4) It is not intended that at the purchase of the property jointly by the Parties hereto nor the terms of this Deed should create a partnership within the meaning of the Partnership Act 1890 or any re-enactment thereof and the parties hereto have agreed to enter into the declaration to this effect hereinafter appearing

NOW THIS DEED made in pursuance of the said agreements WITNESSETH as follows:-

1. IN pursuance of the said agreement set out in Recital 3 hereof it is hereby

declared that the parties shall hold the said property upon trust for themselves as beneficial tenants in common in the following shares namely:-

Practitioner A	three eighths
Practitioner B	three eighths
Practitioner C	two eighths

and it is hereby declared that:-

a) on a sale of the property the proceeds of sale shall be divided between the parties in accordance with the shares set out above

b) for the purposes of clause 10 hereof (option to purchase provisions) the above shares of the value of the property shall apply

c) the above shares shall not apply to a division of the rents and profits of the said property which are to be dealt with on the terms as set out in clause 5 hereof

2. THE parties hereto being the trustees of the said property shall have full power until the expiration of a period of eighty years from the date hereof to sell mortgage charge lease or otherwise dispose of the said property or any part thereof with all the powers in that behalf of an absolute owner

3.(a) IT is hereby agreed that the expenses relating to the day-to-day running of the property such as (which list shall not be deemed to be exhaustive) payments in respect of heat light telephone general rates water rates property insurance occupiers' liability insurance and the proportion of the service charge payable under the terms of the said lease which relate to the day-to-day running of the property and those day-to-day expenses relating to decoration maintenance and repair of the property shall be discharged in equal shares by the said parties

(b) IT is agreed that the parties shall discharge payments in instalments under the mortgage as and when they become due in equal shares

4.(a) IT is hereby agreed that decisions relating to the alteration decoration maintenance and repair of the property if and when required shall be decided by a majority vote and for these purposes it is agreed that out of eight votes deemed to be shared between the parties Practitioner A shall be deemed to carry three votes and Practitioner B shall be deemed to carry three votes and Practitioner C shall be deemed to carry two of such votes

(b) IT is hereby agreed that the expenses involved in connection with alteration decoration maintenance and repair of the property being those which are regarded by the parties as such as are likely to be increased or diminished the capital value of the property including that proportion due under the service charge payable in accordance with the terms of the lease shall be borne by the parties in the following shares:-

Practitioner A	three eighths
Practitioner B	three eighths
Practitioner C	two eighths

if any difference shall arise between the parties resulting from the definitions of the terms contained in paragraphs (a) and (b) of this Clause the matter shall be referred to arbitration as provided by clause 10 hereof

5. IT is hereby agreed and declared that the gross amount arising from the letting of the property or any part of the property shall be shared equally between the parties hereto

6. FOR the purpose of the preceding clause hereto the parties shall open up an account with the Right Bank plc of Newtown for the purpose of the receipt of the rents or profits arising from any letting or licence of the property or part of the property

7. THE parties shall be entitled to carry out their respective professions in the property provided that such use falls within the category of natural complementary or alternative and preventative medicine and providing that such use is in accordance with the planning permission granted by the Newtown District Council without let or hindrance from the others and it is hereby declared that Practitioner A shall be entitled to use the property for two and a half days a week Practitioner B shall be entitled to use the property for two and a half days a week and Practitioner C shall be entitled to use the property for two days a week for such purposes

8. THE parties hereby agree to employ X Chartered Accountants of Newtown or such other accountant as they may from time to time agree to allocate the expenses between the parties in accordance with this agreement and that such allocation shall form the basis of expenses of the property for the purpose of showing in each of the individuals' profit and loss account as prepared for their sole trading purposes

9. IT is hereby declared that it is the intention of the parties that neither this agreement nor the co-ownership of the property shall be deemed to create a partnership under the terms of the Partnership Act 1890 or any re-enactment thereof

10.(a) if any of the parties hereto wish to dispose of his or her share in the property (hereinafter called 'the outgoing party') notice in writing shall be given by the outgoing party to the other party or parties (in this clause referred to as 'the remaining party or parties') recording the outgoing party's desire to dispose of his or her interest in the said property

(b) if the remaining party or parties give notice in writing within fifty six days after receipt of the notice referred to in sub-paragraph (a) hereof of their intention to purchase the share of the outgoing party then this agreement and the notice shall constitute a contract for the sale and purchase of the share of the outgoing party at a price to be calculated in accordance with sub-paragraph (c) hereof and the National Conditions of Sale Twentieth Edition shall apply thereto with completion deemed to take place twenty eight days after the service of the notice by the remaining party or parties to the outgoing party

(c) (i) if notice is served by the outgoing party prior to 1st August 1992 the purchase price shall be that amount by which the outgoing party's share set out in paragraph 1 hereof is proportionate to the sum of Sixty Thousand Pounds (£60,000)

(ii) if notice is served by the outgoing party on or after 1st August 1992 the purchase price shall be that amount which the outgoing party's share set out in paragraph 1 hereof is proportionate to the market value of the property as at the date of the outgoing party's notice

(iii)for the purpose of this sub-clause 'market value' shall be deemed to be the best price reasonably obtainable on a sale at arms length with vacant possession of the residue of the term of the lease of the said property no regard being had to any goodwill of the business carried on at the said property but taking into account the value of fixtures and fittings situated thereat

(d) if the parties have failed to reach agreement of the amount properly representing the market value of the said property within one month of the outgoing party's notice the outgoing party and remaining parties shall appoint an independent expert to determine the market value of the property whose decision shall be final and binding on the parties hereto and in the event of the parties defaulting in agreement as to an independent expert such expert shall be appointed by the President for the time being of the Royal Institute of Chartered Surveyors

(e) on completion the outgoing party shall discharge one third of the amount owing to Healthy Bank plc under the terms of their mortgage dated 1st August 1990 as at the date of completion

(f) the outgoing party shall bear the legal costs and disbursements in connection with the transfer of equity including the fees if any of the experts appointed in accordance with sub-paragraph (d) hereto

(g) notices shall be deemed validly served provided these are sent by recorded delivery to the private address of the remaining or outgoing party as the case may be

(h) if after the expiry of fifty six days from the service of the outgoing party's notice the remaining parties have not served a counter notice under the terms hereof or at such earlier time as the parties have mutually agreed the property shall be placed on the open market for sale and the legal costs and disbursements and Estate Agents commission shall be borne by the parties hereto in equal shares

(i) in the event of the purchase by a continuing party of the share of the outgoing party and there being two remaining parties hereto a memorandum shall be endorsed on this deed of the shares in which the continuing parties shall be deemed to hold the said property

(j) the parties acting accountants shall draw up to the date of completion an income and expenses account for the purpose of allocating the fees received and expenses incurred between the parties and the costs of the preparation of this statement shall be borne by the outgoing party

11. THE day to day running expenses referred to in Clause 3 hereof shall be paid from the account opened with Right Bank plc of Newtown referred to in Clause 6 hereof

12. ANY dispute or question in connection with the terms of this agreement shall be referred to a single arbitrator to be appointed by the President for the time being of the Royal Institute of Chartered Surveyors under the provisions of the Arbitration Act 1950 or any statutory modification or re-enactment thereof for the time being in force

IN WITNESS whereof the parties hereto have hereunto set their hands and seals the day and year before written

SIGNED SEALED and DELIVERED by the)
said Practitioner A in the)
presence of:-)

SIGNED SEALED and DELIVERED by the)
said Practitioner B in the)
presence of:-)

SIGNED SEALED and DELIVERED by the)
said Practitioner C in the)
presence of:-)

COPY WRITING AND DESIGN SERVICE

Whether you are writing advertisements, leaflets or designing your letterhead, image and logo, Hyden House Limited can offer you a complete professional copy writing and design service. From start to finish, Hyden House can assist you with the whole or any part of your project. From conception to printing, Hyden House's broad experience in this field will ensure the best impact and most suitable image for your products or services.

Write to:

Hyden House Ltd
Little Hyden Lane
Clanfield
Hants, PO8 ORU

or telephone:
0705 - 596500

or fax:
0705 - 595834

IS THERE A BOOK IN YOU?

Hyden House Limited are always interested in
projects for new books.

If you have an idea for a book you wish to
write or think needs to be written, please don't
hesitate to send us a synopsis in the first
instance for our consideration.

Who knows, you may just have a bestseller
on your hands!

IF SO,
Write to:

Hyden House Ltd
Little Hyden Lane
Clanfield
Hants, PO8 ORU